Designing Aspen

Designing Aspen

The Houses of Rowland+Broughton

PA PRESS

PRINCETON ARCHITECTURAL PRESS · NEW YORK

Contents

Foreword

Tom Kundig, FAIA, RIBA

In a place where nature verges on perfection, architectural interventions must acknowledge their position within the larger context. They must give way to their surroundings, touching lightly and carefully on these special landscapes. Over two decades of practice in Aspen, Colorado, Rowland+Broughton has developed an approach that is deferential to the environment—creating a modern interpretation of Rocky Mountain architecture that delicately balances built form and nature.

I often say that residential design is the origin of all architecture; home is our essential shelter, and shelter, food, and water constitute the necessities for human life. Home is a place of refuge, memory, family, and tradition. The ten residential projects featured in this monograph demonstrate a keen sensibility of the human scale and a deep interest in how people experience place. They draw attention outward and upward, creating sensory opportunities in which we are acutely aware of the larger landscapes that surround us, while paying homage to the rich history and tradition within the small mountain town of Aspen.

Spending their lives in the dramatic, expansive Rocky Mountain landscape has taught R+B not to be intimidated by its grandeur but to understand the role of architecture within it. They address this drama with nuance and subtlety, crafting experiences where architecture is the vessel for an intimate connection to place. R+B's contextual approach is humble yet bold, continuously adding layers in the evolution of their built identity to carry forward and complement the Aspen Idea—a convergence of mind, body, and spirit.

Preface

Aspen, Colorado, the place where we live and work, is a small Rocky Mountain town with big ideals and aspirations. Having been drawn to the stunning natural environment, vivid history, and abundant culture, we thrive on the richness of a life lived outdoors and total immersion in an extraordinary artistic and intellectual community. Our connection to Aspen is complex, long-standing, and deep. We've always felt that the town elevates and inspires all who embrace its spirit, and that is what we've tried, day by day, to do.

We began Rowland+Broughton in the shadow of Aspen Mountain, sitting across from one another at our kitchen table, a tabula rasa in every sense. Today, twenty years later, practicing in a lovingly preserved historic wooden storefront building on Main Street, with another studio in Denver and outposts across the United States, we felt the moment had arrived to take stock—to reflect on the character of what we've accomplished and what continues to drive our creative approach.

Perhaps inevitably, our "design thinking" is bound up with a profound sense of place. And so for this, our first book, we have selected ten residential projects that suggest the diversity of ways in which a life in Aspen and its surrounding environs can be enjoyed and experienced. We work on multiple project types, including hotels, restaurants, and unique commissions that defy easy classification. But at R+B's core lies a passion for creating homes. We love the opportunity to connect with our clients, to create contexts for living well and making memories. The residential scale is human, a situation in which every detail matters and experimentation is essential. Most of all, it is an opportunity—an honor—to be invited to help people reimagine their lives, and the reciprocal collaboration is lasting and inspiring.

Inherent in these projects is a deep understanding of, and respect for, our place on the map. Each home merges the residents' dreams with site, landscape, views, and light to shape a sublime and singular coexistence. Art is everywhere, from that which hangs on the walls (and the walls themselves) to the mountain views, aspen forests, and elk-filled meadows. Our task is to integrate all of these art forms, both the natural and the human-made, without applying a preconceived style, letting the personalities of the owners, the land, and the context determine the narrative. Together with our clients, we create "convergent" architecture that is meant to last, and to carry forward what has become known as the Aspen Ideal—a unity of mind, body, and spirit.

Aspen has touched us with what came before, what is here now, and what is to come. Thus, even when we embark on something new, we're

thinking about historic preservation and how it affects the "footprint" of our work. We value and respect each site so that it continues to flourish in tandem with nature, harmonizing our clients' aspirations with the surrounding context in a positive, mutually contributing manner. This readiness is rooted in constant curiosity about what our responsibilities are today and will be in the years and decades to come.

We are exceptionally fortunate—blessed, you might say—to have found not only a profession that we love but a place to practice it that brings out the best in what we do and, by extension, who we are. The wellspring that is Aspen is a mix of many things, some apparent, others subtle and even secret, and as we drink from it, we never quite know what the effect will be. But that is the best kind of nourishment, and we hope that as you consider the work in these pages, you'll find that Rowland+Broughton is giving back, in our way, to the town from which we have drawn so much strength, inspiration, and joy.

R+B's restoration and redesign of the 1904 Aspen Times building (left) and the 1889 Hotel Jerome (right)—both iconic representatives of the town's storied history—demonstrate the firm's talent for, and commitment to, maintaining the pleasurable simultaneity of past and present. A new multiuse central courtyard and addition draw both structures into a unified public experience.

Introduction

Spending even a brief amount of time with John Rowland and Sarah Broughton, principals of the Aspen, Colorado, architecture firm that bears their names and is now entering its third decade, one is struck most of all by their seemingly limitless vitality, the racing engine of a young, fun couple with a bottomless curiosity about, and appetite for, life in all its permutations. Thus it is ironic that the term this supremely of-the-moment pair employs to describe the signature quality of their practice—"convergent"—is most accurately explained by a concept dating from the mid-nineteenth century and popularized by the composer Richard Wagner: the Gesamtkunstwerk, a creative endeavor characterized by the convergence of multiple disciplines, alchemized into a seamless, cohesive entirety.

To be sure, the architecture of Rowland+Broughton expresses a clear, consistent vision characterized by a melding of vernacular, modernist, and contemporary styles; a strong connection to landscape, context, and place; the use of light, materiality, and views as fundamental tectonic building blocks; and most of all an exquisite sensitivity to thresholds, a balance between spaces defined (or not defined) by transparency, flow, and permeability. Yet Rowland+Broughton would never describe themselves as visionaries—that is, practitioners possessed of a highly personal, proscriptive philosophy to which everything and everyone must remain subservient. Rather, what might be described as R+B's style emerges from the braiding of interpretation (of their clients' wishes) and collaboration (with multiple disciplines). Thus the architects' essential talent lies in experiential and aesthetic orchestration: bringing together art, design, craft, landscape, and the dreams and ambitions of their patrons into a modern-day Gesamtkunstwerk while remaining generous, open-minded participants.

Not surprisingly, Rowland+Broughton cite as a major influence (both stylistically and as a model of collaboration) a modern Gesamtkunstwerk, one close in spirit to R+B's own integrated approach: the 1957 Miller House in Columbus, Indiana, arguably the high-water mark of US mid-century residential design. Inspired by Mies van der Rohe's Barcelona Pavilion, architect Eero Saarinen crafted an open, fluid plan enclosed by glass and stone; to Saarinen's pristine pavilion, interior designer Alexander Girard added whimsy, color, pattern, and texture (Girard also suggested the living room's famous "conversation pit"); and Dan Kiley landscaped the thirteen-acre site, crafting three zones, each connected to a different part of the house. Led by Saarinen, the first among equals, "these three great creative spirits worked together to make something unique, timeless, livable, beautiful, and delightful," Broughton says. "We come back to that house on a weekly basis." R+B likewise maintains lively involvements with artists, artisans, decorators, craftspeople, builders, and landscape architects—teams that, as the following pages reveal, produce joyful convergences of remarkable richness and cohesion.

If there is a presiding spirit hovering above R+B's efforts—and, indeed, Rowland+Broughton's energetic lives—it is Herbert Bayer, the Austrian-born, Bauhaus-trained creator who moved to Aspen in 1946 at the instigation of the town's great benefactor, Walter Paepcke, and envisioned Aspen itself as an integrated work of art. As an architect, fine artist, graphic designer, visual communicator, and urban planner, Bayer helped to bring into balance the three components that give Aspen its singular personality—mind, body, and spirit—and create what Rowland+Broughton would describe as a convergent town.

Over their two decades in practice, these partners in work and life have knitted together a design concept of an interdisciplinary collaboration and an urbanistic concept of an interdisciplinary town, and applied the combination to the art of architecture. The outcome is a studio that is both highly unusual and part of a great continuum. By carrying forward a tradition and moving it into the future, Rowland+Broughton has produced an enduring body of work—one that, house by house, grows ever more rich and rewarding.

ASPEN

We have a pair of friends who live much of the year back East, in homes one would describe, architecturally, as classical. Their vacation getaway in Aspen, however, is anything but. It's a 6,000-square-foot, twelve-level psychedelic fantasia created in the early 1970s by a Polish-born local entrepreneur, who hand built this Gaudí-esque paean to sex, drugs, and countercultural freedom out of beat-up wood, moss rock, colored glass, and anything else he could lay hands on that captured his already well-stoked imagination. The house is outrageous, hilarious, sublime, the ultimate one-off—and not where you'd expect to find folks who are, like their East Coast dwelling, fairly traditional. But what can we say? Aspen does that to you.

We see it again and again. One of our clients camped out with her husband and three children in an eccentric one-bedroom folly we fixed up for them while their new home was going up. Another commissioned a vernacular pavilion to display art, host soirees, and enjoy tea ceremonies. These, like many local residents, are serious, highly accomplished, sophisticated people whose lives elsewhere belong unmistakably to the world of grown-ups. But Aspen invites—indeed, encourages—experimentation, self-expression, and uninhibited eccentricity. And as architects, life partners, and individuals, the two of us wouldn't have it any other way.

How did Aspen get like this? In part, its character can be traced to its origins as a Wild West boomtown inflamed by lodes (and loads) of silver. From 1879 until 1893, it experienced the kind of runaway prosperity that provokes great leaps of infrastructural progress. Two railroads, the Denver and Rio Grande and the Colorado Midland, brought in the eager-to-strike-it-rich multitudes, and Aspen became the first town in the West to enjoy electric street lighting. When you look at photos from that period, you notice the paucity of trees—so many were cut down to put up new structures and shore up the mining tunnels. School-building, and the opening of the Wheeler Opera House, the Hotel Jerome, and the first Aspen Mountain tramway, spoke to the presiding sense of optimism, and of permanence.

The 1893 repeal of the Sherman Silver Purchase Act, which demonetized the precious metal and incited a "silver panic," blew it all away. Aspen entered a decades-long decline the locals still call the Quiet Years. People took apart their shacks and decamped with the timber. Amid the vacant lots, the remaining structures sold for cheap, and the phrase "ghost town" wasn't an overstatement.

Two things transformed Aspen's fortunes and, braided with the adventurous spirit that got the place moving in the 1870s, produced the town we know and cherish today. The first was the realization, beginning in the 1930s, that Aspen was the perfect place to practice a then up-and-coming sport: skiing. This was abetted during World War II by the arrival of the 10th Mountain Division at nearby Camp Hale specifically to train for military maneuvers in difficult mountain environments. So enamored of Aspen's skiing conditions were the soldiers that they returned after the war and started building chalet-style lodges.

The second fortuitous occurrence was a 1945 visit from Walter Paepcke, founder of the Container Corporation of America, instigated by his wife, Elizabeth. Blown away by what they

found, and envisioning a forward-looking paradise in which mind, body, and spirit might flourish, the Paepckes launched the Aspen Idea, creating—along with much else—the famous Aspen Music Festival, the Aspen Institute, the Aspen Center for Environmental Studies, and the International Design Conference. Perhaps the Paepckes' masterstroke was bringing in the Austrian creative polymath and Bauhaus alumnus Herbert Bayer to oversee the town's resurrection. Bayer distributed gallons of Necco wafer–esque paint colors to residents and encouraged them to splash them about liberally, and helped promote the ski boom (which roars on today unabated) with his iconic posters, which equated a run down one of Aspen's now-legendary slopes with fun, thrills, and glamour.

Aspen, without question, can seem like a rarefied paradise in which to spend time. But it is the "mind, body, and spirit" sensibility that prevails, and that drew us here—along with the astonishing, never-gets-old beauty—a quarter century ago. Back then we were in New York, and highly appreciative of the density and humanity and culture on offer as well as our proximity, as practitioners, to design professionals at the very top of their game. But we'd both gone to school in Boulder, Colorado, and we missed the easy availability of incomparable nature, the hiking, biking, and skiing, and the heady cultural component for which Aspen remains justly famous.

Honestly, we've never looked back. We have knitted ourselves into the community—personally, as architects, and culturally. And the adventurous, curious, idiosyncratic approach to life—a quality at the core of the Aspen Idea—is something we enjoy and embrace. Day by day, it enriches and nourishes the totality of our existence.

Dreamers once came to Aspen to dig for silver. Today, the place is a gold mine of ideas, individualism, and natural wonders, in an atmosphere devoid of judgment on which we all thrive, and for which we are all most grateful. Right now the challenge is to manage growth, to not make it all about consuming and continuing to get More, but rather nurture the kind of balance that will enable other Sarahs and Johns to come here and have their own versions of the blessed life we lead. No one says it'll be easy. But if any place has the elasticity to pull it off, it's Aspen.

Meadow House

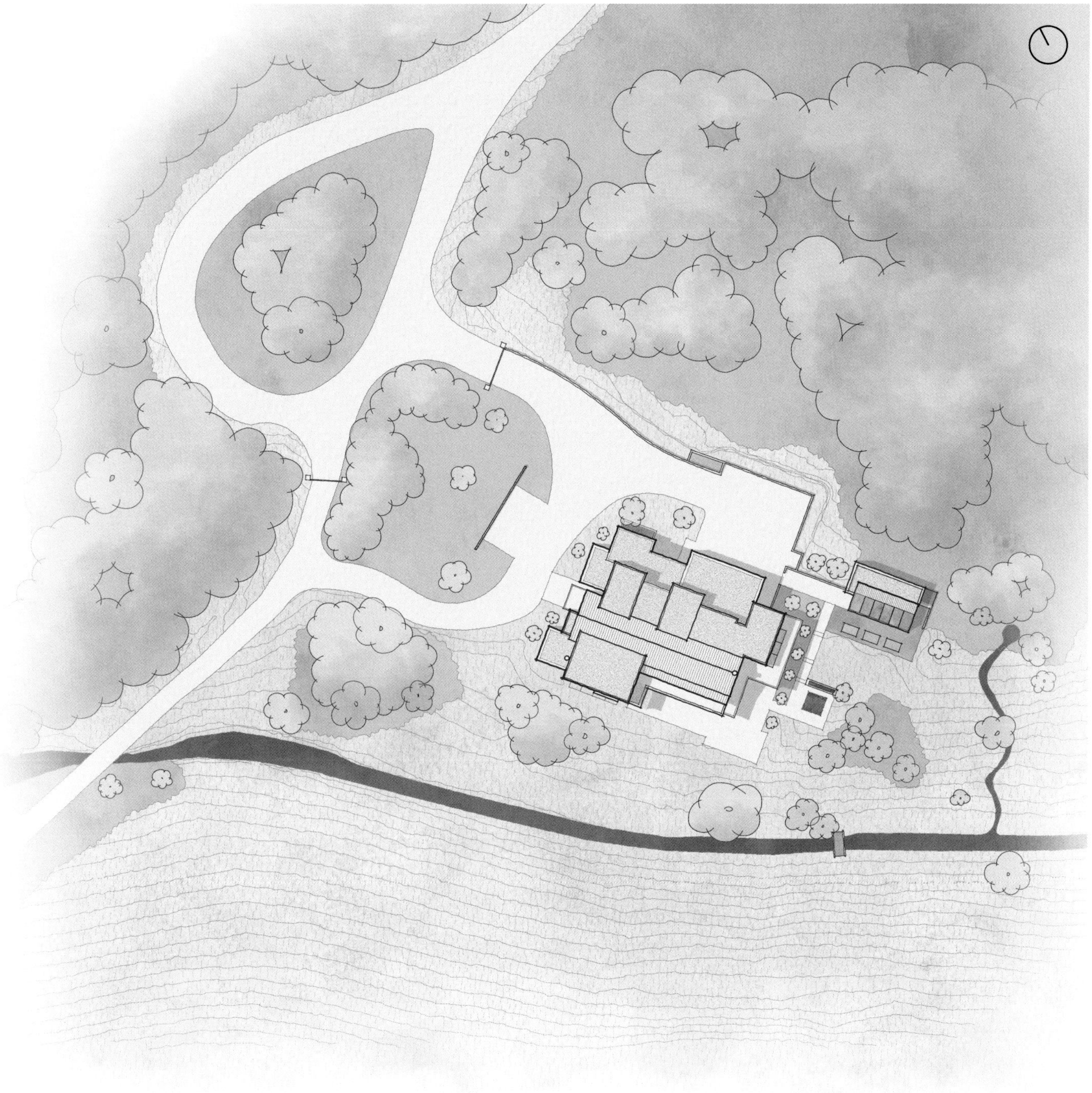

One of the enduring tenets of classical modernism (to coin an oxymoron) remains "form follows function": the belief that the outside of a building, rather than being drenched in unnecessary and misleading ornament, should reflect its interior. R+B's Meadow House, so named for its siting on an expansive greensward ringed by evergreen, spruce, and scrub oak trees, turns this foundational dictum on its ear. On approach, the structure reads as an agglomeration of black-and-white boxes clad in wood, stone, and metal, all supporting a standing-seam peaked roof. Nothing about this arrangement, however, prepares one for what lies beyond the threshold. And Meadow House, in conception and execution, could not be more modern.

When discussing the project, R+B tends to emphasize a particular element found on the second floor of the residence's meadow-facing side: an "agrarian gable form," as Broughton describes it, that gradually "peels upward" as it moves toward the house's eastern end, revealing progressively more of the view. One understands the architects' pride in the gesture. But it is worth noting that it slightly mischaracterizes the design: the gable remains the only vernacular component in what is otherwise an entirely contemporary dwelling. Nor it is foundational to the project's story. Rather, the essence of Meadow House lies in the idea of the threshold: between separation and connection, public and private, interior and exterior. "Where to draw the line?" is a question that runs through all of the firm's work. Here, R+B has answered it with the utmost discernment, elegance, and drama.

Though the three-level, five-bedroom dwelling could hardly be characterized as small, the eleven-foot ceiling heights and enormous glazed walls of the main floor's public rooms make Meadow House feel considerably larger than its 8,500 square feet. The sense of abundance is further amplified by the residence's style. The knotty wide-plank bleached spruce floors and light oak of the ceilings and casework call to mind the grand yet spartan villas of Scandinavia. And, too, the fact that there are no hallways to speak of. The spaces seem to dissolve into one another in a subtle experiential unfolding.

This narrative of rooms that are discrete yet interconnected stands as the architecture's most notable achievement. On the main floor in particular, the visual connectivity, the plan's porosity, is remarkable. From the entry hall to the living room to the kitchen to the combination library and dining room (for "a client who is a consummate reader," Broughton observes, "this is the hub of the house"), the sense is of a grand loft space with no hard barriers interrupting the flow. Yet at the same time, each room has its own particular character. If the overall experience seems holistic, the component parts nonetheless feel distinct and discrete. Given that the nearly full-height glass sliding doors can open the rooms to the landscape almost completely, R+B has pulled off a neat trick: an authoritative work of architecture that remains magically on the edge of dematerialization.

The architects have struck a similarly fine balance in the separation of public and private spaces. The house belongs to a woman with three children, someone at once deeply involved with family life and actively engaged in business and philanthropic pursuits. Accordingly, she required, within this very interactive domestic environment, her own domain, and the architects obliged with a zone that is effectively a house within the house. On the main floor, just beyond the dining room, R+B set the client's office, which adjoins a full bath with ample dressing and closet space, making it suitable for a bedroom conversion should the need arise. They then secreted, within this zone, a concealed spiral

page 30:
The outcome of R+B's close collaboration with the client is a house that holds art, architecture, and landscape in a well-judged balance.

opposite:
Among the house's most notable features: the alternation between a muscular materiality and a nature-embracing transparency.

overleaf:
On the second floor, R+B emphasized what Broughton characterizes as "an agrarian gable form" that "peels upward" as it travels toward the view.

stair that rises into a dressing room at the heart of a second-floor primary suite. Thus the owner enjoys her own de facto duplex at the house's eastern end, and can retreat to or emerge from her private quarters without having to pass through the public rooms via the main stair.

Meadow House also puts on display R+B's integrated approach to art, which here involves collaborating with makers to create a nexus between design and architecture, and weaving a formidable existing work into the structure itself (as opposed to the more usual approach of finishing the walls and hanging pictures on them). Regarding the former, the Los Angeles–based Haas Brothers' whimsical, organic, double-sided mantelpiece enlivens both the living room and the adjoining study. The latter centers on a remarkable three-dimensional collage by artist Tom Molloy, which combines a series of individual protests into a comprehensive cri de coeur against a multitude of global injustices. Originally displayed in a gallery setting on a long shelf, R+B reassembled the piece in two layers, enclosed it in a vitrine featuring integrated lighting, then inserted the entirety into a wall in a long, narrow zone opposite the bar, where it can be the focus of close study and proper appreciation.

As noted, the membrane separating the interior from the great outdoors is slender in the extreme, and Meadow House's permeability remains highly seductive, whether the meadow itself is a field of green hosting a herd of elk or a blank slate of snow broken only by the thin, tawny line of a split-rail fence. From a view standpoint, the peel-up gable, rising toward the southeast as it travels the length of the primary suite—achieving liftoff as its sweeps past the corner windows of the bedroom and seems to bank toward the distant mountains—stands as the design's iconic moment. But there is an additional viewing experience that is separate from the house itself: a greenhouse, sited above the back lawn off the residence's eastern corner. The shed, made of glass, steel, and stone, was designed, according to R+B's mission statement, "for a year-round edible garden and [to] enable a farm-to-table learning experience for the family." But the greenhouse also acts as a viewing machine, offering a different, and no less panoramic, way to absorb the property, meadow, mountains, and great Western sky.

One of the dwelling's more surprising thresholds was created not by the architects but by their client: the balance between furnished and void space. This is most notable in the living room, part of which features a conventional arrangement of sofas and chairs while the rest has been left empty—space to be enjoyed for its own sake. "Just because you have the room doesn't mean you have to put chairs there," Rowland observes. "It's a pause. There's power in that."

In fact, a narrative of what constitutes true power (as opposed to force) has, in Meadow House, been most revealingly unspooled: power expressed as intercommunication rather than separation; the ability to choose engagement or solitude without compromising one or the other; and boldly imagined architecture that remains welcoming of, and humbled by, the natural world. The design suggests that there can be as much strength in deference as in self-assertion. It's a great deal to ask of what is, enfin, a home. But at Meadow House, R+B has achieved it.

More Solitude

opposite:
The house's finely balanced porosity is evident in the pass-through between the dining room/library and the kitchen, which also affords a view of the main stair.

above:
For this bibliophile client, R+B created a dining room that serves, as well, as a library.

above and opposite:
A spiral stair, concealed behind double doors, in the main-floor office connects to the second-floor primary suite dressing room.

above and opposite:
The primary suite's comprehensive glazing reveals two notable features: a private terrace and a trapezoidal clerestory shaped by the ascending roofline.

South Elevation

opposite and above:
The hardscape elements that gently demarcate the exterior sitting areas remain both spare and sculptural, shaping space suggestively without separating the precinct of the house from its natural surroundings.

above and opposite:
The main stair, at once spartan (in its use of plain pine boards) and grand (in its gracious scale and elegant geometries), unites all three floors of the residence.

Mountain Retreat

The national park lodges built in the late nineteenth and early twentieth centuries remain among the nation's most beloved buildings: they represent a moment in history when, with the frontier on the brink of extinction, Americans engaged, many for the first time, with the natural splendors of the West. But there is also the style in which they were built: the soaring log atrium of the Old Faithful Inn, with its towering central fireplace; the Ahwahnee in Yosemite, a surprisingly refined blend of wood, stone, and Native American art and artifacts; El Tovar, with its views of the Grand Canyon from the South Rim—these and other hostelries conflate the rustic and the grand in a manner so distinctive that it became its own genre, known affectionately as "parkitecture." The lodges had two critical missions: to connect their guests with nature, visually and experientially, and to encourage a sense of community and conviviality in which chance encounters with strangers could blossom into friendships, both short- and long-term. Thus did design as an engine of social connectivity lie at the core of the lodge, and help to define an emerging nation's social character.

As it happened, Mountain Retreat was commissioned for an Aspen property in an area known for strict design guidelines that reference national park lodges as architectural templates. Says Broughton, "We wanted to create a modern house for modern family living." Yet it occurred to R+B that the open, convivial character of a park lodge was, in fact, not such a bad precedent on which to draw. And not only in the obvious places—for instance, the public rooms, where family members might be expected to gather—but also in the interstitial zones like hallways and stairs, in which unexpected meetings tend to proliferate.

The property also invited a strong connection to nature. Located in a forest of aspen and fir trees at the base of the Aspen Highlands ski area, with conversation-stopping views of the Maroon Creek, Roaring Fork, and Hunter Creek Valleys and their surrounding mountains, R+B foresaw an indoor-outdoor experience in which rooms opened onto private and communal exterior spaces, which in turn embraced their incomparable surroundings. The outcome, though modern in plan, detail, and connection to the site, would capture the expansiveness, and incomparable majesty, of the Western landscape that characterized parkitecture's golden age.

R+B dealt with the multitude of approvals the design required (entitlements, as they're known locally) with an expeditiousness born of two decades of Aspen building experience. The site itself, however, offered a greater challenge, as the land was steeply sloped, and bookended above and below by public roads. "So we had to create a plinth—a buildable lot—and a driveway that was at an appropriate grade for snow," Broughton recalls. Thus was the location of the drive dictated by the relative flatness of its entry point and visual connection to the street. Six months were consumed by a monumental shoring effort to create a level building site (also known as a "bench") and the massive retaining wall that holds back the hill on the property's north side, which sinks to a depth of forty feet and against which the house is set. "And this was all," Broughton adds, "before we could begin construction."

The ease with which this modern lodge commands the location, its natural sense of belonging, belies the arduousness of the sitework. This has in large measure to do with the elegance of R+B's adaptation of the park lodge style—their simultaneous adherence to and transgression of the district's design guidelines. "How do you create a glass box in a neighborhood that wants 'national park'?" Broughton asks. The answer: the volumes visible from the street draw materially on a traditional

page 60:
The vertical elements flanking the front door and the window directly above it recall film sprocket holes, reinforcing the notion of the house as a viewing machine.

opposite top:
The broad hallway and habitable stair encourage not only art appreciation but unexpected encounters among family members and guests.

opposite bottom:
The living room enjoys a cozy intimacy and, via wall-size sliding glass doors, unfettered communication with the spectacular site.

vernacular, including irregular stacked stone walls, rough-hewn horizontal wood siding, and a standing-seam metal roof, while the elevations not on public display feature floor-to-ceiling glass walls and pocketing transparent doors that utterly erase the divide between architecture and nature.

One of the most distinctive, and consistent, features of the firm's work is its tectonic translucence—the architects' talent for connecting rooms while also maintaining their discretion—a bit of spatial sleight of hand that makes their plans feel at once gloriously open and invitingly cozy. This motif is used to especially appropriate effect on the house's main floor. Entering via an oversize pivot door, passing a grand stair that offers visual connection between all three floors, one passes through a broad, wood-lined portal and finds virtually the entirety of the house's communal experience on display: the living room, with its expanses of glass framing Aspen's iconic mountain views; the outdoor entertaining area and, just beyond it, the pool deck; and the dining room, lightly separated from a gleaming white kitchen illuminated by an upsloping, fourteen-by-sixteen-foot skylight (there's a green roof as well, over the living room). If one of the defining features of the great national park lodges is their welcoming embrace—the sense, upon entering, that an adventure is about to begin—then R+B has reinterpreted that quality of pleasurable anticipation at a domestic scale.

Given the nonhierarchical program—the idea that everyone would be, in this house, on an equal footing—R+B eschewed the usual primary suite, opting instead for four bedrooms and a bunkroom. Yet it might be more accurate to say that each of the private quarters offers a suite-style experience. All of the rooms are accessed via a buffer zone that serves as a decompression space between the public hallway and the sleeping/living area, and all feature banquettes with trundle beds, allowing adults another way to read and relax (there are built-in desks as well) and young children to sleep in their parents' rooms. The self-contained character of these spaces—their well-equipped privacy, augmented by corner windows and private terraces—makes for an appealing contrast with the communal areas, offering each family member and visitor a comfortable, bespoke escape.

Curiously, for a 10,750-square-foot, three-level home that can be enjoyed in so many different ways (the lower floor features a gym and game room), the most magnetic areas are the interstitials, the hallways and grand stair. Partly this derives from that quality of translucence, the blurred boundary between a room and that which adjoins it. But this appeal derives primarily from capaciousness. The hallways are wide enough to be comfortably inhabited (some feature window seats), and the stair, with its thick wood treads akin to benches, remains an experience unto itself, floating between the various levels, affording views up, down, and across a realm of changing moods as well as perspectives. Somehow, the theme of the architecture—the meaning of the experience—hangs in the air of these areas like a mist. They are zones of opportunity, of the unexpected sodality emblematic of the park lodges in their prime, reinterpreted for the present day.

Ellsworth Kelly

ITA ACKERMANN
Olafur Eliasson

Campbell's
CONDENSED
CHICKEN NOODLE
SOUP

above and opposite:
R+B created discreet, cozy sitting areas in the graciously scaled hallways (flooded with natural light), increasing the house's utility and encouraging the notion of space at once social and intimate.

overleaf:
Each of the bedroom suites is separated from the public hallway by a brief entry zone, thereby increasing a sense of tranquility, and is augmented by corner windows and, in this case, a private terrace—both embracing natural light and expansive views.

Lookout House

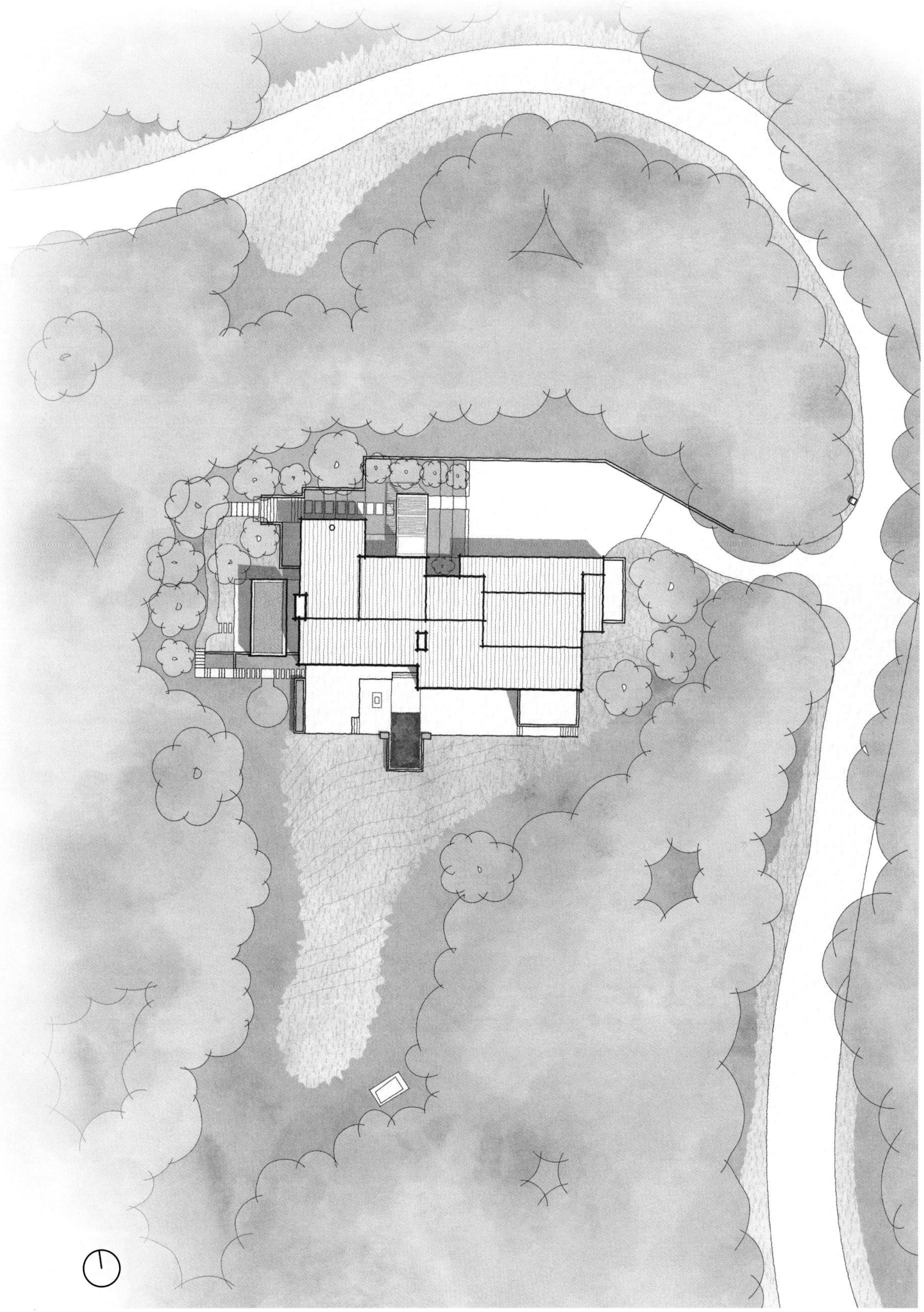

It can be an intriguing exercise to mentally reverse engineer a design: to unpack an architect's intentions, understand the various motivating factors, and observe how these threads have been woven together into a cohesive entirety. Lookout House, an 8,700-square-foot dwelling commanding a steep site and enjoying sweeping views of Aspen's Elk Mountains, offers just such an opportunity. The house occupies the footprint of the owners' previous residence and is roughly the same size. But in its responses to the particular character of the location, the needs and predilections of the residents, and indeed the aspirations of the architects, Lookout House could not be more different from its predecessor.

Though many of R+B's residential projects benefit from their surroundings, the location here is particularly unusual. The site overlooks a broad, deep, dramatically down-sloping meadow that, as it is densely forested on each side, remains invisible to the neighbors (who are in turn invisible to R+B's clients). Thus the view is both astonishingly grand and utterly private, a singular combination anywhere, but particularly so in the Aspen mountains. Given the circumstances, R+B perceived two opportunities: to make the house a portal to the meadow, and to maximize the building's visual engagement with the drama of its surroundings.

Regarding the former, the architects chose to directly connect the north-facing entry facade to the house's southern elevation, which overlooks the view. An axis beginning at the oversize pivoting front door extends directly through the house to a massive pocketing glazed panel on the south facade, a window that opens onto a mountain-filled vista and, a few steps below on the deck, a copper spa pool. The effect is stunning, a bold gesture that effectively lays a T onto the plan, with the interior axis dividing the residence almost perfectly in two and meeting a series of interconnected deck spaces that extend the full length of the structure's south side.

As for the latter challenge—capturing the slope—the architects crafted what might be described as an upside-down house. They set the secondary rooms on the lower level (with the guest bedrooms to the east of the axis and the family room, game room, bar, study, and gym to the west), and the primary spaces upstairs (living, kitchen, and dining rooms to the west, and a monumental bedroom suite on the east side), where they enjoy views that, beginning far below at the bottom of the meadow and traveling up, up to the distant mountain peaks, are pleasurably commanding. Fortuitously, the site slopes upward to the west, so that even though the second floor, as Rowland puts it, "hovers over the landscape," the living room opens directly onto a covered dining terrace with an accompanying outdoor kitchen.

Unusually for Aspen, the house's parti suggests a sensibility akin to the modernist grandeur of postwar urban architecture. Given the near-museum scale of the owners' contemporary art collection, the choice remains entirely appropriate, and R+B's approach to the style unfolds in unexpected ways, particularly in a residential context. This is encapsulated in a powerful gesture at the house's center: a floating stair, at once dramatic and feather light, that ascends from the entry to a translucent landing on the second floor, exquisitely detailed in glass, wood, and a long expanse of perforated steel.

If there is a dominant design motif, it is horizontality. Floating planes and, in particular, layered plinths transform in function and character as they slip from space to space, at once defining rooms as discrete entities and uniting them into a single interlocking experience. The exterior canopy that shelters the entry walk finds an echo in the

page 88:
The house's entry experience elegantly combines the local vernacular (horizontal barn board, standing seam metal roof) and a contemporary sensibility (expanses of mullioned glass, a modernist steel canopy).

opposite:
The entry hall, accessed via a pivoting front door, offers encompassing views of the first and second floors, and is flooded with natural light from double-height glazing.

overleaf:
A soaring space, the first-floor den is overlooked by the living areas on the second floor and draws in daylight from the exterior stair on the front of the house, just past the entry.

covered outdoor seating area at the house's west end. The flamed granite that forms a banquette in the kitchen transforms into cabinetry as it moves into the dining room. The plinth that supports the stair leading down to the primary bedroom turns a corner and becomes the room's hearth. These and other gestures infuse the house with an overlay of simple elegance, and unite a complex program into a paradigm of cohesion.

Various qualities prevent the home from feeling too gallery-like. The first is—even for a firm known for its porous designs—an unusually high level of visual connectivity from room to room and, indeed, floor to floor. This begins, appropriately, at the beginning. From the entry, the eye travels, virtually unimpeded, through the glass panels enclosing the stair, falling upon the main-floor game room, the upstairs living room, and the art wall on the second-floor landing (also enclosed by glass). The living room overlooks the double-height space of the family room, shares space with the dining area, and connects visually to the adjoining kitchen. And virtually every room in the house captures panoramic views. The outcome is a rich, reassuring awareness of the presence of others, of a residence vitalized by daily life.

Lookout House is also made welcoming by the fluidity of its restrained palette, which morphs from concrete to oak to limestone to leather as it flows from space to space, connecting to the house's exterior materials and the natural world beyond. Above all—and most unusually for a modernist design—the dwelling conveys an overwhelming sense of craft. "Everything in this house was custom-designed," Broughton affirms. "Everything. Not only did we design the beds, we even made the pillows. It was an incredible opportunity."

It can be tempting to pigeonhole R+B as a New Regionalist firm, one working largely with the building blocks of a Rocky Mountain vernacular. In fact, Lookout House's weathered barn siding and standing-seam metal roof suggest, at a glance, a fidelity to the local architectural sensibility. Even from the motor court, however, the shoji-like expanses of mullioned glass and International Style entry canopy begin to dispel the regionalist implication, and taking two steps past the threshold demolishes it completely. The dwelling is in every way a modern house—one that reflects the rigorous and consistent predilections of its creators.

EAT DRINK NAP
FROM ABOVE

opposite, above, and left: The architects' graceful use of slippage to create fluent connections between zones remains evident in two intercommunicating rooms: the granite framing the banquette in the kitchen transforms, on the opposite side of the spaces' common wall, into the structure of the sideboard in the dining room.

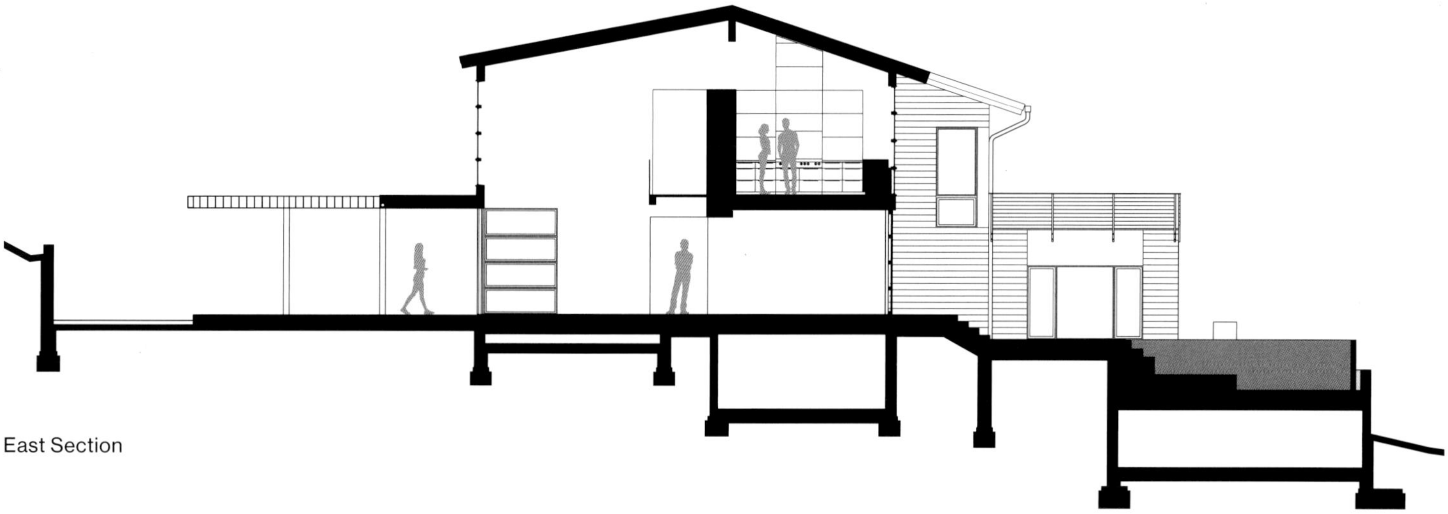

East Section

pages 102–3:
An axis extends from the front door to a monumental pocketing glazed panel on the house's opposite side, a window that opens onto a south-facing view and a copper spa pool.

opposite and overleaf:
Architecture meets nature in the landscaping, which unifies, facilitates, and softens the exterior connections between the house's levels and nestles the structure firmly into its sloped site.

HISTORIC PRESERVATION

If you're an architect in Aspen, you should be into historic preservation.

R+B has been *very* into it since we set up shop two decades ago. We've both held positions on multiple boards, commissions, and organizations devoted to good stewardship of Aspen's heritage and its future. John signed up with the Planning and Zoning Commission and the Urban Infill Commission. And Sarah coauthored the City of Aspen Historic Preservation Design Guidelines and spent eight years on the Historic Preservation Commission, the last two as chair.

You learn a lot, and not just about the task at hand. You meet different kinds of people. You find out how things work, and don't work, in this very special, very singular town. Sitting on boards and commissions teaches you grace and diplomacy, as many of the projects you review were designed by your friends and colleagues. Most of all you learn to be succinct, to not fall in love with the sound of your voice but rather to get your point across in less time than it takes to soft boil an egg and keep things moving. Quite apart from cultivating a deep and fine-grained understanding and appreciation of Aspen's architectural gems (and how they were cut and polished), our involvement with historic preservation has made us abler practitioners and more generous individuals.

Our particular take on the subject is on display for all to see at our studio in the landmark 1889 Mesa Building, so called for its situation at the high point of Main Street, six blocks from the heart of town. Its style, massing, and details are all representative of an indelible moment in time—the architecture perfectly captures Aspen the boomtown, when silver was king—and so, on the outside, we put the building back to what it was. We returned the windows to their original double-hung configuration, restored the front porch, and left the initials that old-timers carved into the exterior woodwork visible beneath the new paint. On the inside, however, we opened up both floors and the basement to accommodate the needs, and the style, of a twenty-first-century architectural practice. Past and present meet in the entry, where we installed our in-house café opposite the reception desk, behind big, historic storefront windows that embrace the street—an inviting transparency that, from its origins to the present day, expresses Aspen's essence.

The Mesa Building reveals the big ideas behind both our work in historic preservation and the renovation or rehabilitation of less august structures: figure out what works, bring it forward, and expand and elaborate on it; eliminate the accumulated wrong turns and miscues; and infuse the totality with program that answers the present-day, and hopefully foreseeable future, needs of the residents. In both situations we engage in a kind of archaeology, performing in-depth research and analysis, coming to terms with the parameters established by what is preexisting and by context, and developing a hierarchy based on how our clients live and how they want to live. But we seldom approach a project thinking that everything has to go. The baseline is: "This is good—now how can we make it great?"

Something else we've learned: excavating the history of a *family* stands as an act of preservation. Our clients, like the homes they choose to buy, have things in their lives that work and don't work, and figuring out how to preserve and enlarge the components that are authentic to their DNA, and extract the parts of the human house

opposite:
The house's unusual double brise-soleil mitigates sunlight and heat gain in all seasons.

above:
To the right of the living room fireplace, a large pocketing glass door—an R+B signature, seen here in closed position—helps to effectively dissolve the distinction between interior and exterior.

Though wood-burning elements are prohibited by Aspen's building code, the house's four active fireplaces—two of which appear in the kitchen and the living room—predate the ordinance and so were preserved in R+B's renovation.

above:
Sited at the approximate center of the plan, the kitchen reflects the house's felicitous interweaving of old and new, as well as its artfully layered spaces, which overlook one another and the outdoors; the room relates, on one side, to the living room and to the children's craft room (with its large interior window) on the other.

overleaf:
R+B repurposed the original house's glulam beams, strengthening the link between old and new. Another example: at one end of the eight-foot-wide hallway, the entrance to the primary suite is guarded by the former front door, imported by Stein Ericksen from his native Norway.

above, right, and opposite:
The primary suite—incorporating two preexisting wood-burning fireplaces, one in the bath—takes full advantage of the view via wall-filling glass sliding doors.

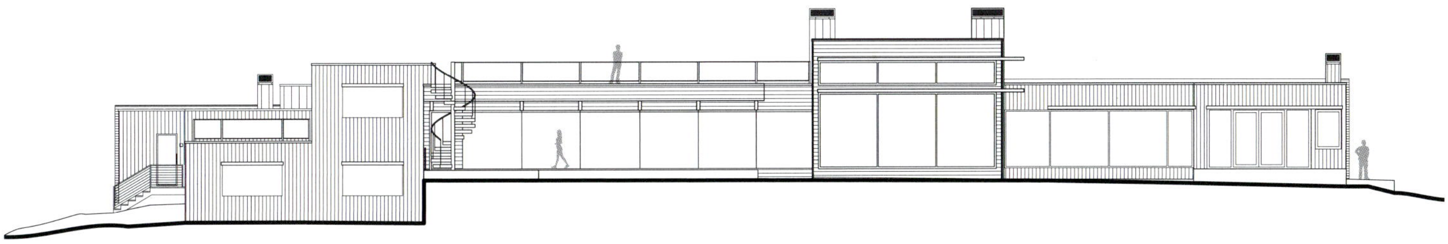

West Elevation

opposite, above, and overleaf: In contrast to the front facade, composed of light gray stone, the side and back elevations are dark in color—both to minimize the architecture's competition with its surroundings and to emphasize the house's near-complete transparency on its view-facing elevations.

While renovating a building may seem to offer less opportunity than a blank slate, a considerable creative challenge is detonated when the preexisting component is picturesque: a relic or ruin, ideally dating from a bygone, colorful age. Then, all manner of possibilities come into play. There is research into the building's history or, if that history remains unknowable, speculation about how the relic might have been used (or, in extreme cases, what it might have been). Yet perhaps the most interesting line of inquiry for both client and architect is how the old might become a part of something new—the structural and emotional interplay between the vivid past and the practical present, and how the two can complement and contrast in an equipoise that addresses both contemporary programmatic demands and the romance of history. "The past is never dead," wrote William Faulkner, memorably, in *Requiem for a Nun*. "It isn't even past." So goes the vibe in the most effective hybrid homes.

R+B's Barn Studio—one of their smaller projects, at just over 3,000 square feet—rings a most interesting change on the idea of the new-old house. Perched on a ridge in Aspen's Starwood district, it appears to be a remnant of a mostly collapsed, rubble-stone agrarian structure, curved on one side, reconceived as a residence via the insertion of a contemporary component: a ground-floor living/dining area beneath a sleeping loft/library, with double-height glazing on the view side and eccentric, crescent-shaped kitchen and bath spaces tucked into the curve. But it is nothing of the sort. The building is entirely modern, created by its original owner as a kind of contemporary folly and designed to precisely resemble a clever meeting of modern life and the golden days of Colorado's yesteryear.

The architects' clients, a couple with three young children, purchased the house and its abundant surrounding acreage, seeing it as the cornerstone of a compound that would in time include a range of building typologies, including a grand family home. The idea was, on the one hand, to make the folly habitable for five people while the other structures took shape, and, more significantly, to create a paradigm for building, and living, on the site, a blending of past and present that respected and embraced the area's rural-agrarian history while extending that legacy into the moment and, indeed, the future. Thus was R+B tasked with creating a different sort of new-old house: a hybrid that preserved the original's eccentric character and the spirit in which it was conceived while also preparing to expand imaginatively upon the foundational idea.

Barn Studio unfolds on three levels, one of them windowless and subterranean. In what was previously the domain of a gym and bedroom with a distinctly "swinging pad" personality, the architects replaced one of the spaces with an unexpectedly elegant media room—its screen faces a long, crescent-shaped upholstered banquette—and made the former bedroom into a game room. On the double-height main floor, a few steps down from the entry foyer, R+B brightened the palette: sanding and bleaching the wood-paneled walls and parquet de Versailles floor, replastering the walls, inserting a steel rectilinear mantelpiece, lightening and contemporizing the compact curved kitchen. The L-shaped mezzanine received a Murphy bed and additional bookshelves to form a de facto library area that is a cousin to, rather than a copy of, the preexisting casework on the main floor. Although there are abundant reminders of the studio as it was—notably a distinctive carved ram's head motif on the stair banister and bookcases—the outcome is at once more useful and more cheerful. It is a welcoming, offbeat hideaway that feels a part of the past but not mired in it.

"The five family members would stay here when they came to visit," Broughton recalls. "They'd all crash in the loft." Of the two residences that followed Barn Studio on the property, says the architect, "I think they're informed by what we did here first—there's a textural quality to them. It's all about stewardship. Uniting the past with today's processes while respecting and appreciating the people who were here before."

The World of Ornament
TASCHEN
LIVING IN STYLE PARIS
ANIMAL WORLD by Chopard
DECADES A Century of Fashion
CAMERON SILVER

pages 138–39:
Seemingly a repurposed ruin, Barn Studio is in fact an entirely contemporary structure—a modern folly.

opposite top:
The building is an exercise in exposure and concealment. The view from the living room's mezzanine (pages 146–47) presents a humbling Arcadian panorama, whereas a subterranean space is snug, self-contained, and divorced from the great outdoors.

opposite bottom:
Materials and details both old and new emphasize the space's warmth and its eccentricity.

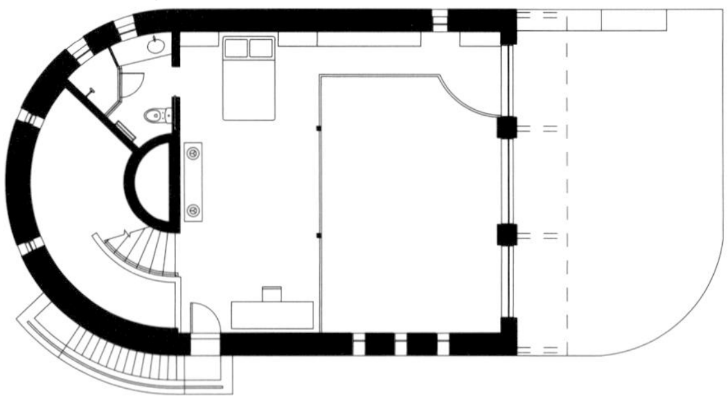

Upper Floor

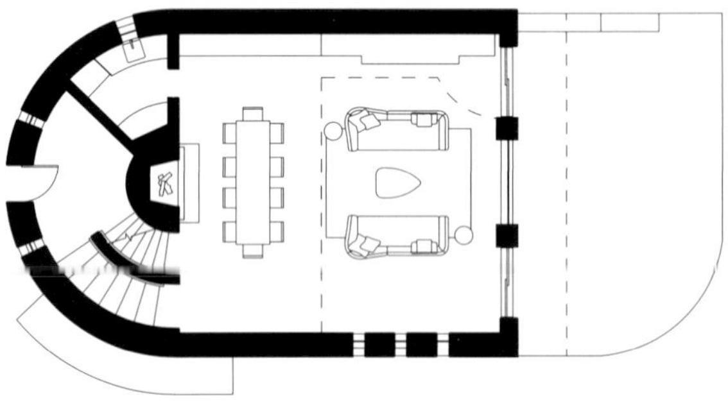

Main Floor

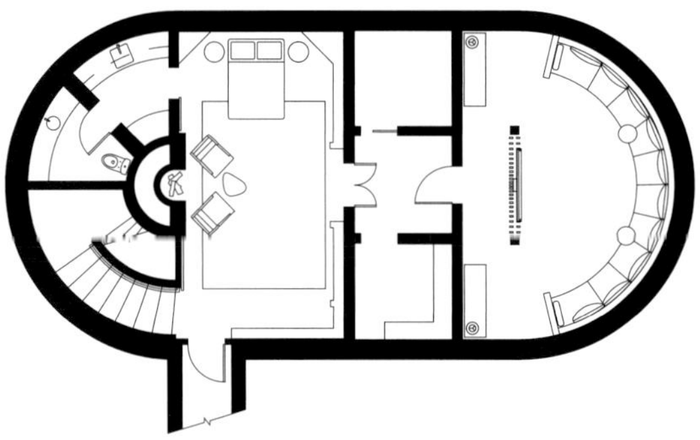

Lower Floor

LITERARY AUSTIN

CLIENTS

In 2023, as part of a celebration of R+B's first two decades in practice, we created a gallery installation of sorts in our studio, featuring pinups of projects spanning twenty years. The response we received caught us somewhat by surprise: many people, looking at the work, concluded that there was no such thing as a consistent R+B "style." Rather, each building was a singular response to a different set of circumstances and the particular needs of the client.

There are, we presume, as many approaches to the architect-client dynamic as there are architects and clients. At R+B, we tend to shy away from individuals who completely disengage from the design process. Rather, recognizing that being allowed into someone's life is a gift, we prefer to pursue committed creative relationships, which enable us to achieve a deep understanding of our clients' desires, so that the architecture we give them stands as the fullest possible expression of who they are and what they envision. Thus it might be said that the R+B "style" is responsive and engaged rather than predetermined or exclusionary. Our passion as architects is for an iterative process, wherein the outcome isn't what we decide you should have, but rather a house reflective of your dreams. It is a humble rather than an arrogant journey that's not about us, but about a realization of an individual's or a family's aspirations.

The central component of a creative relationship—no matter the medium, but maybe especially in architecture, given the scale and complexity of what you're undertaking—is getting to know your collaborator, with the work and the relationship revealing themselves, hand in glove, as the experience progresses. This is perhaps particularly the case with the homes we realize in Aspen, not infrequently for people with strong, clear (and clearly stated) viewpoints, and personalities to match. One of the virtues of experience is that you learn to listen for the good idea, to recognize when a client has gone down a path of inquiry that is especially promising and may take the project in an exciting, unexpected direction. Of course we have strong opinions. But it's been consistently the case that if a client adamantly refuses an idea, even one we're certain is the right way to go, it's an opportunity for something else to emerge. Our creative mantra has always been "good to great," and that transcendent leap of quality requires an extra measure of thought, patience, and effort.

It's very important to add that while we are friendly with our clients, we never forget that R+B is a service provider. We know our place and behave in a professional manner at all times. That said, there is sometimes a desire on our side to deepen the connection, to become true friends. It has much to do with the companionable, small-town character of Aspen, where you tend to run into interesting people, attend the same events, ponder similar questions big and small, and share comparable interests and, indeed, eccentricities. Making something together is an excellent way to start a relationship. It begins professionally, and if it remains that way, so be it. But we're always pleased if the connection continues and evolves, opening a welcome new chapter and enriching our lives. That's *really* good to great.

For the owners of the Barn Studio, R+B revivified an existing pool house, bringing it into aesthetic balance with the project's residential component.

Art Barn

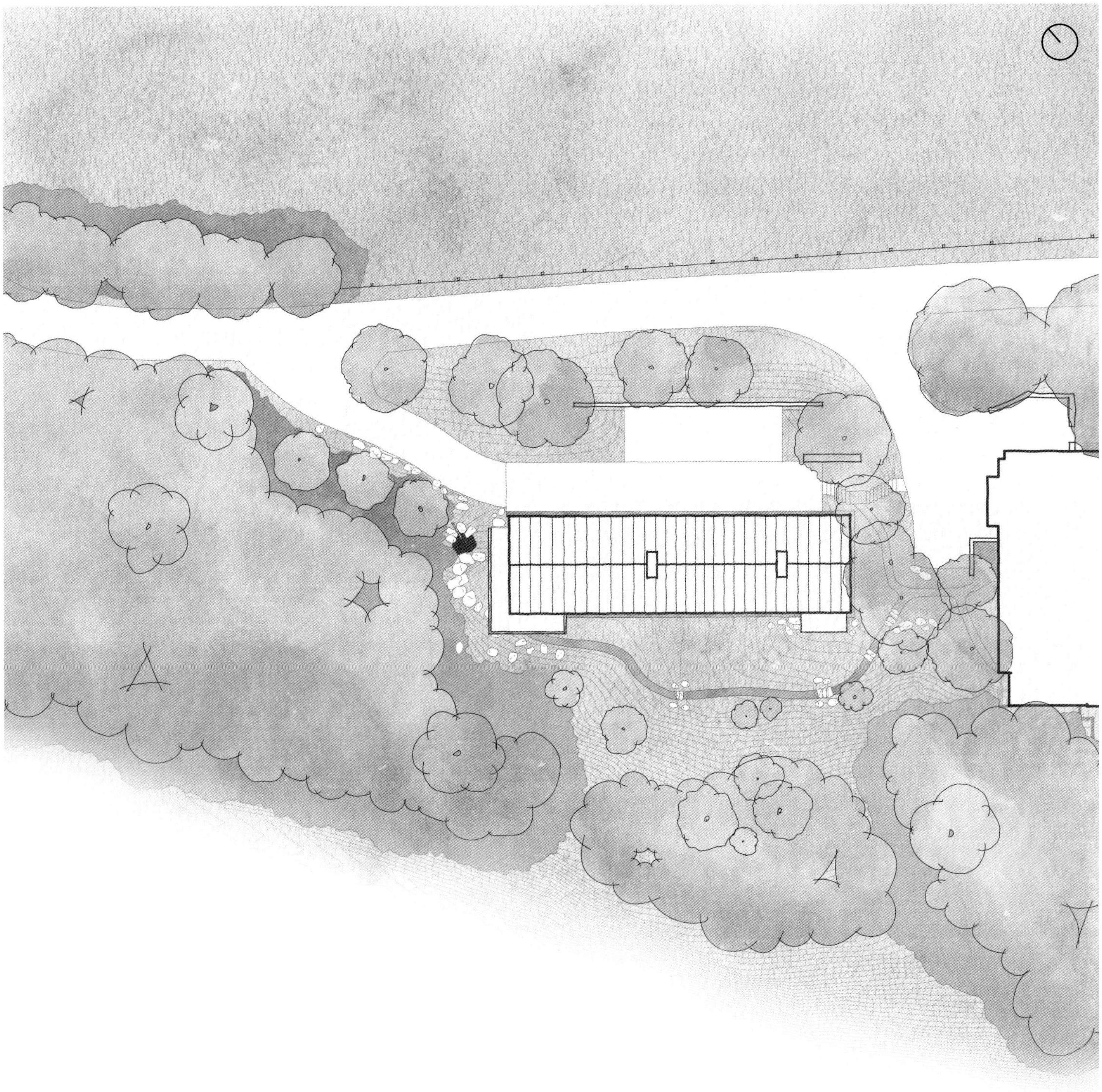

Many, if not most, of R+B's residential projects enjoy spectacular views, and this one, on Red Mountain, is no exception. The CinemaScope windows, one of the firm's design signatures, reveal a palette of the locale's iconic peaks and slopes: Independence Pass, Aspen Mountain, Aspen Highlands, Buttermilk. "And on a clear day," says Rowland, gesturing toward the horizon, "you can see the fourteen-thousand-foot mountains beyond."

Yet as regards the world past the windows, the 6,200-square-foot Art Barn remains unique. So compelling is the experience of the interior that the panorama becomes a backdrop rather than a focal point. The irony is that the architecture could not be more spare. What commands one's attention is not flash but purity.

The architects first engaged with their clients on the adjacent site, when they were asked to modify an existing chateau-style residence the couple had purchased. Over time, however, the couple's interests began to outgrow their home. As their art collection expanded to include not only wall-based works but also sound and video installations, they required an environment in which to showcase new pieces. And as their already fervent engagement with the local community, national and international art worlds, and the social, intellectual, and political issues of their times escalated and enlarged, the pair needed a place to host get-togethers and events: a combination art and music venue, think tank, and salon. It was a singular program, one that demanded a no less special place to nest.

What their clients had in mind, the architects learned, was a rural structure—an "intimate and understated, vernacular idea," Rowland recalls. The object took shape as a 113-foot-long gable form, topped by a corrugated zinc roof and clad in charred cedar. Within, the material palette is strictly limited to oak, plaster, limestone, and concrete. Perhaps inevitably, "as the project kept going, it became a little more refined," Rowland notes. In fact, the building suggests a smaller residential variant of Herzog & de Meuron's Parrish Art Museum in Water Mill, New York. But Rowland cites a different influence: "We were drawing on John Pawson."

Art Barn's simplicity is actual but also, in a sense, thematic. There is a front door, signaled by a split rock welcome mat set into the cobblestone motor court and a screen composed of horizontal wood slats, but the facade remains deliberately nonhierarchical. There are four identical sliding glass panels (which disappear into the eighteen-inch-thick walls) that permit entry into the house at different points along the front elevation, quietly demolishing the idea of "making an entrance." Here, the architecture seems to say, is a space devoted to art, community, and ideas, not ego.

The interior continues this deference to matters of the mind, soul, and spirit via a comprehensive commitment to the pristine. "The word we used was 'austere,'" Rowland recalls. "We edited and removed things that were unnecessary. We went to great lengths to not have any outlets or switches on the primary walls." On the main floor, comprising a great room, video gallery, office, kitchen, and primary suite, "all of the floorboards are custom sized. They vary within an eighth of an inch, and continue, unbroken, almost from end to end," reflective of a desire to create a perfectly crafted object. On the lower level, the province of two additional bedroom suites and more gallery space, R+B exposed and finished the poured-concrete foundation wall, creating an expanse of utilitarian elegance. There is also what might be described as aural austerity, thanks to the thickness of the walls.

Though set up to serve as a living/dining space—with a minimum of judiciously selected and artful

opposite:
Choosing to shape a nonhierarchical entry experience, R+B designed the front door as one of four identical portals, distinguished by a wood-slatted privacy screen and a stone "welcome mat."

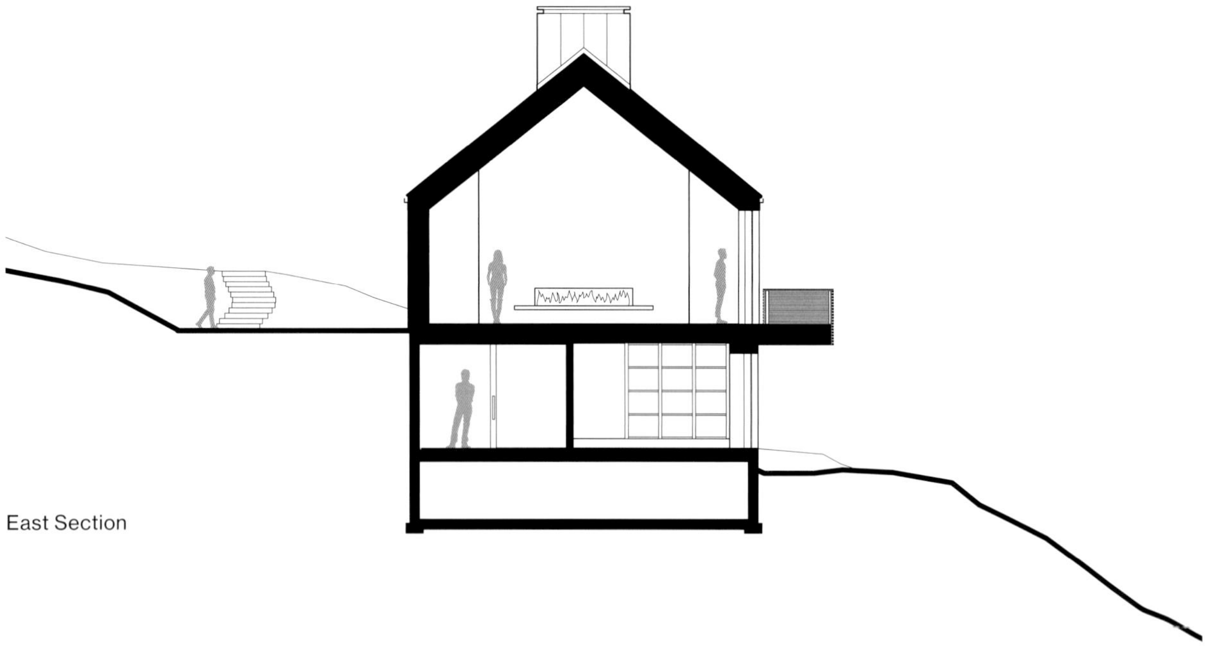

East Section

furnishings, notably, end tables by Donald Judd and a runway-size carbon-fiber dining table that seems to dissolve, at midpoint, into the incoming sunlight—R+B designed the great room to be maximally accommodating, the better to host get-togethers at every scale. The architects also took pains to make Art Barn art-friendly. One long wall showcases Sol LeWitt's *Wall Drawing #578* (2010, painted in situ like all such LeWitt works) and a mobile by Björn Schülke that responds to movement within the room. For both the upstairs and lower-level galleries, "we worked with a video art consultant from New York, so that, depending on what an artist chooses to present, you can have multiple screens and different sound sources," Rowland explains.

The project's surprise component—Rowland calls it the crescendo—is the firm's contemporary interpretation of a traditional Japanese tea room, tucked away behind the lower-level video gallery, its full-height sliding-glass corner doors opening the serene space to an exquisite, Asian-influenced mountain garden. The tea room, it might be said, is the servant of two hierarchies and two cultures. There are dual entrances—one for the tea master (which conceals the preparation station), the other for guests—and two spaces, one a tatami room, the other featuring a long, low Nakashima-style table and cushioned poufs for those unused to prolonged cross-legged sitting. In both zones, the elements and materials are firmly rooted in Japan (albeit with red cedar paneling and bluestone pavers representing the Rockies): Arakabe plaster, sliding screens inlaid with shoji paper, and hand-woven tatami mats, all contributed by the clients. The tatami room's traditional "god pillar" is the couple's as well. "It washed up in front of their beach house back East," Rowland explains.

If the tea room extends the everyday into the realm of the ceremonial and even the spiritual, the same might be said of R+B's design. It isn't precious. But the purity of the architects' achievement, their consideration of even the most seemingly inconsequential elements and their contribution to the whole, inspires an unusual level of avid attention. The view is still out there, available at any time for one's delectation. But the serenity and simplicity of the interior exert a potent force—an awareness of the moment that, rather than becoming routine, only deepens with time and experience.

above and opposite:
The living room's absolute simplicity—in which every structural detail is suppressed and sockets and switches are concealed—serves to highlight the space's essential features: light, views, and, uppermost, art.

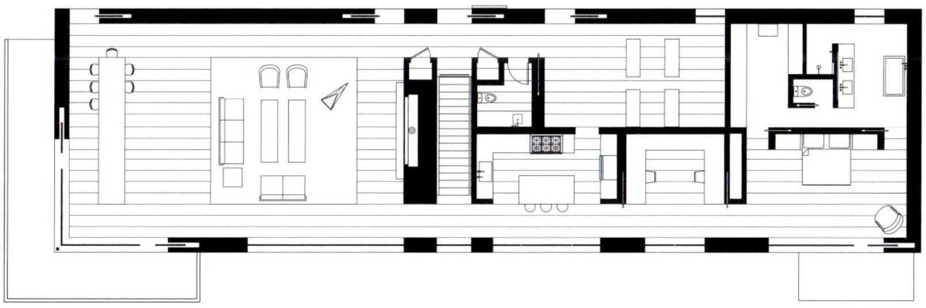

Lower Floor

Main Floor

opposite:
Natural light from the window vitalizes the textures of the stairwell's hand-troweled walls.

above:
The study seems to have been hewn, rather than constructed, from a single material.

left:
A kitchen as pristine and functional as its surroundings.

above and opposite:
The primary suite demonstrates the design's commitment to absolute simplicity in both form and materials. The hanging objects in the bedroom are in fact art pieces; each orb conceals countless small speakers that play symphonic music.

The tea room (above), on the building's lower level, opens onto a Japanese garden (opposite) via glazed sliding doors. Though there is a tatami room, the low Nakashima-style table and poufs enable visitors unused to prolonged cross-legged seating to enjoy the tea ritual in comfort.

Bagua House

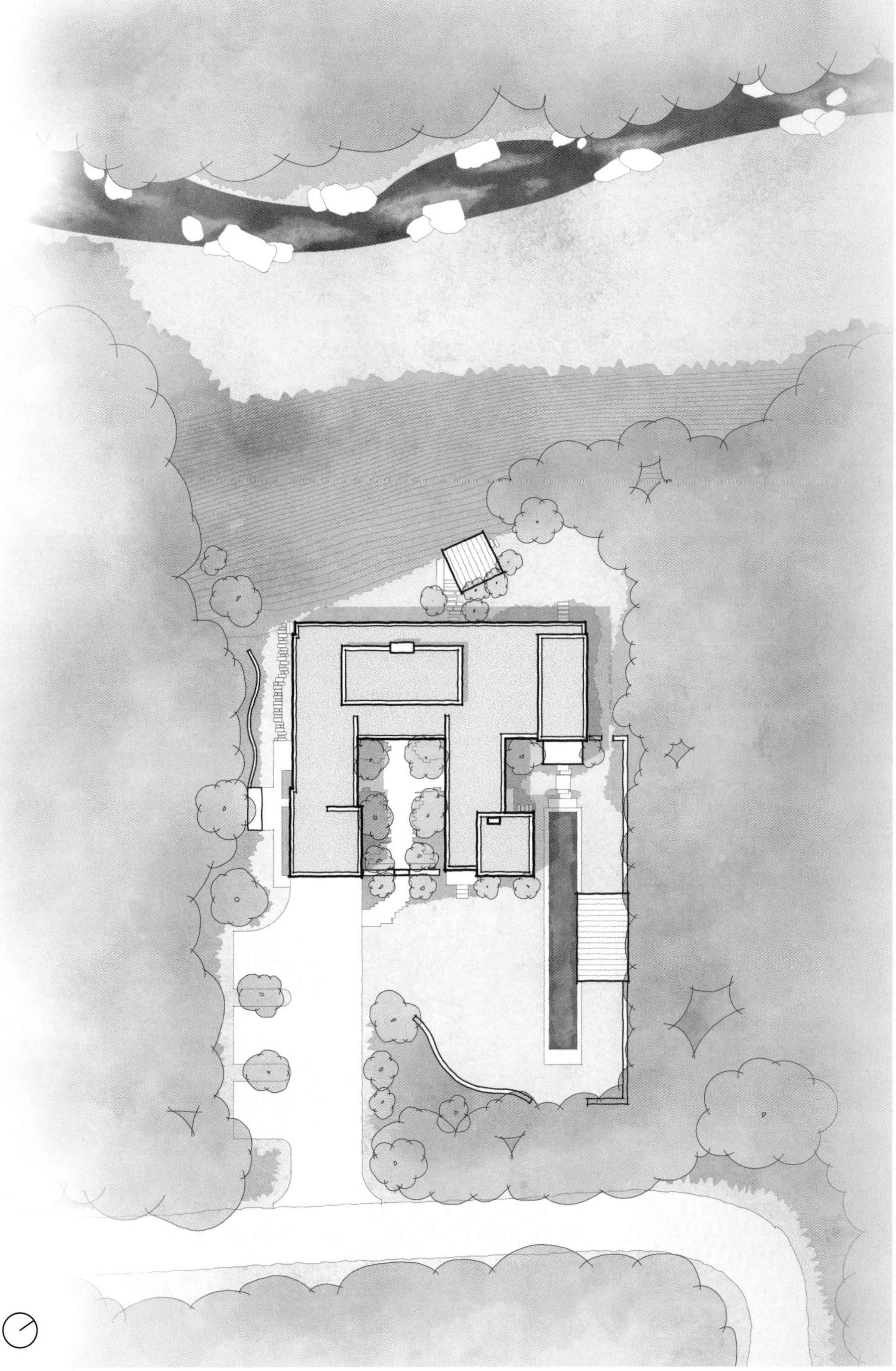

One of the more misunderstood (and improperly pronounced) concepts in the lexicon of architecture and design is feng shui. Translating literally as "wind water," feng shui is an ancient Chinese practice designed to use natural forces to bring structures of all types (including tombs) into harmony with their settings and surroundings, the better to maximize the experience of the buildings' inhabitants, whether corporeal or spiritual. As the translation suggests, feng shui draws on the interrelationship between the seen and the unseen worlds to optimize the connection between our outer and inner lives. Ideally, the five elements at the core of the practice—earth, metal, fire, water, and wood—are represented in a way that produces balance and, consequently, a positive flow of energy within one's built environment.

Feng shui, as practiced in the West, draws typically on the bagua, a set of eight symbols representing different, interconnected aspects of existence. This often takes the form of a bagua map, which, laid over a room, a plan, or a landscape (or all three), helps identify relationships that encourage or impede the various aspects of one's life, the better to support the former and correct the latter.

How precisely Bagua House deploys the principles of feng shui is not overtly apparent. Yet the 8,250-square-foot, five-bedroom dwelling, perched atop a steep slope on a property enjoying various and expansive views, remains highly unusual, in both its approximate U-shaped plan and its relationship to the site. Most of R+B's designs are defined by what might be characterized as public and private permeability, a transparency that at once connects them to their sublime surroundings and, internally, opens their component parts to one another. Bagua House lays claim to the same qualities, but with the difference that, in this instance, interior spaces connect through exterior rooms. This interleaving of inside and outside creates an exquisite sense of amplitude, one that is as much emotional as actual. The ability to look out a window and see, across a courtyard, another wing of the residence infuses the architecture with the drama of the palatial. Yet the main effect—the bagua effect—is soothing and reassuring, as though the structure had internalized the environment, taken the landscape and views into its welcoming embrace and enfolded them into the life of the family.

Appropriately, the heart of the experience is the residence's landscaped entry court, which sits between the three main wings of the plan. Also appropriately, the court has its own front door, a patinated Cor-Ten steel portal on axis with the entrance to the house, flanked by knee-high stone walls, that serves as the definitive moment of transition from the wider world of the site to the intimate experience of the dwelling. The court's design remains a model of discreet intentionality. The lapping of water from fountains tucked into the knee walls bestows upon the house its own aural signature. The miniature allée formed by half a dozen pruned trees (three on each side) gives the arrival experience a quiet sense of occasion. The blend of grass and pavers on the ground and vertical cedar boards and stone on the walls creates an enveloping experience that is part architecture, part nature. And the transparency of modernist full-height glass doors with slender steel mullions offers tantalizing suggestions of the dwelling's domestic character. By the time you reach the oversize charred-cedar front door with its enormous dish-shaped handle, you have been absorbed—with the most finely tuned understatement—into the singular world of the interior.

The house is entered via an attenuated foyer that, with its low ceiling, vertical cedar paneling, and wood portal that replicates the Cor-Ten one outside, serves as an internal extension of the external setting. Thus the double-height living/dining great

page 178 and opposite: The courtyard and living room are linked via a foyer that recapitulates the language of the entry experience and blends with supple ease into the interior.

room, light-filled thanks to high clerestory windows and glass-and-steel doors that frame long views, serves as a pleasurable reversal of expectation. From this grand curtain raiser, a more intimate scale is established in the house's two wings—the long sides of the plan's U, which are accessed from the great room's opposite ends. To the south, the architects set the intercommunicating family room and kitchen—casual and comfortable, open to the landscape on two sides yet cozy and inward-looking. The wing to the north, containing the parents' suite, the three children's bedrooms, and their communal kids' corner, represents an especially felicitous bit of design work. It enables the two generations, though in relatively close proximity to one another, to participate in the landscape in discrete, and very different, ways.

Though the overall plan, as noted, forms a de facto U, the bedroom wing reads as an L, with the primary suite extending in one direction and the children's quarters in another. While the former includes the usual complement of spaces—bed, bath, dressing—its apogee is an exercise room and hot yoga studio that opens onto a sitting terrace and, beyond it, a seventy-five-foot-long lap pool that crosses the lawn's north side and appears to extend into the lush conifer forest beyond the property line. The children's bedrooms, conversely, are accessed by an almost fully glazed hallway (terminating in their common lounge) that overlooks the entry court and bathes the space in abundant southern light.

Bagua House could not, by any means, be characterized as small. (There is also a capacious belowground zone featuring a guest suite, media and wine rooms, and a play area, accessed via an unexpectedly wide "habitable" stair.) Yet Rowland isn't wrong when he cites "the humbleness of this house, the scale and proportion. It's not trying to be any more than it needs to be." The modesty of the architecture does indeed contribute to the residence's beauty and unity. But it is the integration into the landscape—the positive flow of energy characteristic of the successful application of feng shui principles—that gives Bagua House a very pronounced, defining sense of serenity, one that in every particular seems to promote and encourage the practice of wellness.

The composer and virtuoso pianist Frédéric Chopin famously observed that the ultimate goal of his music—simplicity—was the hardest to achieve. It might be similarly said that the highest objective of architecture, also diabolically difficult, is to disappear—to make every choice, every gesture, so natural and inevitable that one perceives, within a successful building, nothing more or less than one's own presence. So it is with Bagua House: a commingling of the built, the natural, and the human that feels at once comprehensive and sublime.

pages 184 and 185:
The grand, double-height living/formal dining room opens into an enveloping den enriched by a warm, medium-hued color palette.

above and opposite:
The kitchen and informal dining/sitting area form two sides of a single space off the living room and open onto the garden, visually and actually, from two directions.

opposite and above:
The children's lounge, at the terminus of a fully glazed hallway that provides access to each of the kids' bedrooms, connects freely with the house's front lawn and its forest and mountain views.

above and opposite:
The architects sought to open the house to its surroundings as completely as possible, in the private quarters as well as the public rooms. The outcome is at once a glorious and calming partaking of the experience of the site and its setting.

ANDO
THE BOOK OF SYMBOLS
HOMES FOR OUR TIME
FRENCH RIVIERA 1920s

opposite:
The multivalent stair descending to the house's lower level serves as a provisional library, a display area, and, upon occasion, a place to relax.

above:
The seventy-five-foot-long lap pool, seen from the "grownups'" exercise room and hot yoga studio.

Creek House

Le Corbusier famously described houses as machines for living. They are also, if well made, laboratories in which to brew emotional interactions—that particular elixir that we tend to refer to as love. This is perhaps especially the case for multigenerational dwellings. As families get bigger and the tree develops more branches, as some members patinate with age and others are newly minted, the notion of a place for all escalates in appeal. Even the most private and independent among us yearn for a residence that is both shelter and gathering place.

Creek House grew out of precisely this impulse. Developing the program, R+B took a novel approach. "There are thirty family members, so we created a mission statement and solicited feedback for what qualities everyone wanted to see in the house," Broughton relates. The architects discovered that, for this particular family, the optimal way to strengthen intergenerational connections was not only to design spaces with highly specific uses but also to enable the people within them to participate in collective activities, break off into smaller groups, or enjoy solitary pursuits. This paradigm of unforced togetherness, it was determined, would encourage family members to seek one another out. The architects reinforced the idea by crafting bedrooms that, if far from monastic, were more suited to the basics (sleeping, dressing) than prolonged periods of isolation. "It was about creating opportunities for people to gather together, but have their own experiences," Broughton explains. The theme was encapsulated in the dining table, which can expand to seat thirty people or shrink to accommodate just a few. "That," the architect recalls, "came to be one of the most significant design elements of the house."

But first, the style. Among the projects to be found in these pages, Creek House is the one most easily associated with a recognizable regional idiom: the old-time Western ranch house. This outcome was not quite as evident as one might assume, given the setting and the circumstances. The house is notably grander than one would have found in these parts in the late nineteenth or early twentieth century. To make it work, R+B developed an exceptionally effective, romantic narrative about how Creek House could be at once contemporary in scale and very authentic. "We decided that we'd found a stone structure—a barn—on the land, and a farmhouse close by it, and connected these two old vernacular buildings with a modern glass link," Broughton says. "And in the link we put the stair and the elevator."

The architects carefully detailed and particularized each of the house's three components, the better to make credible their tale. From the front, the stone volume, which contains the garage and mudroom, reveals three broad, tall wood plank doors, each capped with a roughly chiseled stone lintel and held in place by four wrought-iron strap hinges. None are operable. "They're just there as part of the narrative, to suggest an old outbuilding," Broughton says. In fact, the structure is entered via a three-car garage door in back, also topped by a stone lintel that sags, artfully, at the midpoint. Appropriately, all of the stonework remains shaggy. "It's really hard to get masons to be sloppy," Broughton observes. "You have to say, 'Make it look like it's been here for a hundred years!'"

The glass link, as part of the narrative, incorporates the exterior walls of the stone barn on one side and the wood-clad main house on the other. "We wanted it to feel like you're in this zone between the two different buildings," Broughton says. As for the principal residential volume, though it is more extensively glazed than its counterparts from previous centuries would have been, the weathered horizontal boards, towering stone chimney, and standing-seam metal roof place it indelibly in style and in time. The component that seems to pin the house most

page 204:
The glass "hyphen" connecting the stone-clad garage and wood-slatted residence supports the narrative of two preexisting vernacular structures connected via a contemporary insertion.

opposite:
The door to the glazed linking pavilion serves as one of several entrances and facilitates direct access to the main stair.

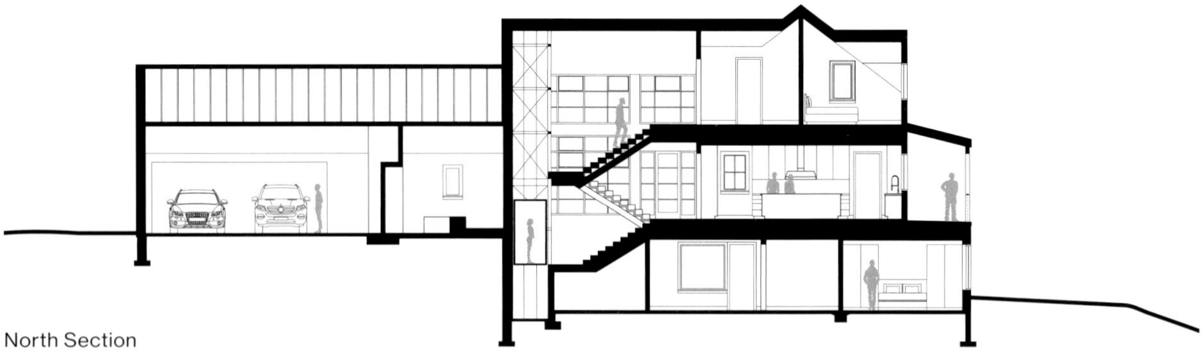

North Section

firmly to a historical moment is the wraparound covered porch, which touches four elevations and—in this sun-soaked, unblemished, spectacularly picturesque, and largely bug-free setting—proves irresistibly inviting even in the cold months.

There are six bedrooms on the upper and lower floors, and play and media rooms (and wine storage) below, but the house's particular multigenerational appeal lies beyond the front door on the main floor. The living/dining/playing/lounging great room, which soars to a height of twenty-three feet and communicates fluently with a bar area and the kitchen, reflects the precise understanding of zoning R+B has perfected in many of their projects. The fireplace is flanked by reader-friendly nooks (with banquettes) beneath sash windows; there are two primary sitting areas, one before the fireplace and one at the room's midpoint; a gaming table stands before a bookcase; and the monumental feasting table lies at the room's far end, just before the pocketing doors that connect to the kitchen. Natural light from dormers, clerestories, and the glass sliders that open the room to the porches and the wider landscape washes the space for virtually the entire transit of the day. The sense of peace—of being at home—is overwhelming, in an environment that can be savored in multiple ways.

In a residence of this nature, one's ability to be intimate with the architecture derives from tactility, your connection to the things you touch. This was perhaps especially the case with Creek House, as the palpable presence of nature—the feel of the trees and grasses, the scents carried on the breeze, even the sounds of the nearby creek and the land's feral inhabitants—sharpens one's desire to participate in the environment. Thus R+B took particular pains with the materials: for instance, treating the ubiquitous oak with different finishes, applying a diamond plaster to the walls, and selecting a pelt-like silver travertine for the baths, yet keeping it all simple. The details, too, are highly particularized, with custom-designed, custom-crafted hardware and joinery that invites the "touch" of the eye.

The experience lends poignancy to the phrase "a work in progress." "These projects take three to five years, and things change," says Broughton. "There's marriage, birth, you name it, it's going on. You have to be a key member of the family without being too involved. There is an art to being a trusted adviser."

above and opposite:
The chalet-style great room draws in light from windows on three sides and was designed to give family members multiple areas—and ways—to engage with one another.

above and opposite:
The kitchen connects to the dining area (with a custom-designed and -crafted table seating a maximum of thirty people) at one end of the great room, spatially, visually in its structural and material details, and via shared lighting elements.

right:
The bar, at the end of the entry hall and just off the living room, expresses a blend of simple vernacular elements and contemporary programmatic pleasures.

opposite and above:
The glass hyphen offers two forms of vertical transportation (the dark shaft holds an elevator) and serves primarily as a transitional zone. Yet it is also a comfortably habitable space in its own right and provides access to the residence's expansive wraparound covered porch.

above and opposite:
R+B deliberately simplified the house's bedrooms to encourage communal activity. Yet the emphasis on the pleasures of solitude and comfort and the thoughtfully executed decorative richness render them exceptionally inviting.

Thunderbowl

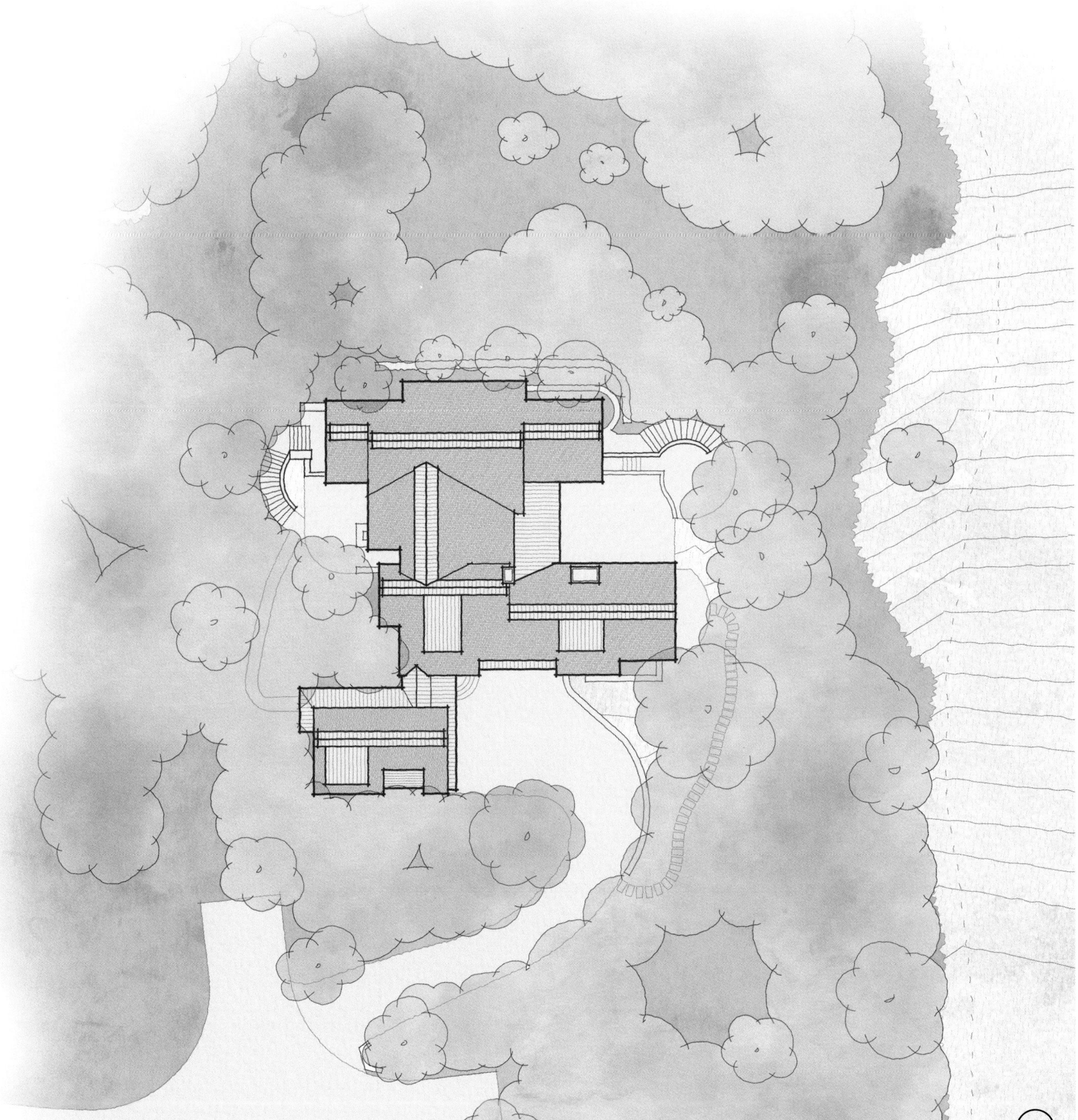

Over and again, a word that arises in connection with R+B's work is "sustainability": in material choices, in methodology of practice, and most of all in the firm's preference for, whenever possible, renovating rather than demolishing existing buildings—one of the greenest of architectural pursuits. Thus it was that at Thunderbowl, an existing alpine mountain house, R+B thought not of wiping the slate clean but rather about what, truly, was essential. "Crucial to our design process is editing," Broughton says. "We start with something and ask, 'What's necessary or needed?' This project was good practice for doing that."

The house takes its name from the exhilaratingly fast Thunderbowl ski run, its next-door neighbor on Aspen Highlands mountain. So close is the slope to the residence that, in winter, one's attention is frequently riveted by the sight of a skier hurtling past the windows. Thunderbowl has a different appeal in spring and summer, when it transforms into a deep-green meadow dotted with wildflowers. "Our clients love it here in all seasons," Broughton affirms. "The house is an incredible way to experience the setting."

In fact, for a 10,000-square-foot dwelling originally constructed by a developer (it occupies a property in Aspen Highlands Village, a mixed-use community completed in 2001 and master planned by Robert A. M. Stern Architects), the place had, in R+B's view, much to offer. The principal challenge lay in the overbuilt interior, with rooms that didn't fluently communicate and structural elements that interfered with, rather than encouraged, light, views, and flow. The residence, in effect, lacked the permeability that is R+B's particular specialty, and the architects were excited by the prospect, not of reinventing the design, but rather of releasing its latent potential.

Though all exterior changes required approval from the neighborhood's design review board—even the new synthetic shingle roof, which replaced fire-hazardous wood shake—the architects' primary intervention, other than removing the extraneous framing and trusses that cut off views on the gable ends, involved the glazing. "We changed swing doors to sliders," Broughton explains, "and every window had mullions, so we extracted them. Also, while evening out the relevant exterior wall, we added a wall-size plate-glass panel in the dining room and enlarged the window above the stovetop in the kitchen—all to bring the alpine in."

Changes to the interior precisely reflected R+B's desire to do only the necessary. "For instance, the lounge space connected to the kitchen," Broughton says. "Originally it was on the living room level"—a few steps below—"and was walled off, so you entered from right off the front stairs. It was a completely separate space. We raised it up to the kitchen level and merged the two rooms," which made the lounge more useful, gave it better light, and tied it to the larger social experience of the house. The stairway connecting the first and second floors had been entirely enclosed, a vast opaque shaft at the house's center. The architects removed the enclosure and replaced it with steel mesh, opening an optical cone between the two stories. A new interior window on the second floor created views from a hallway down to the dining room and, beyond it, the ski slope.

While exposing the rooms and levels to one another, and the entirety to the majesties of Aspen, was the primary objective, R+B also considered the effects of natural illumination on the particular character of the interior. "In Colorado, we have really harsh southern and western light," Broughton observes. "It's beautiful, it's amazing, but it's important to balance it with light from the north and the

page 222:
As part of their redesign, R+B layered sleek contemporary materials and rough-hewn vernacular elements, most notably in the house's main stair.

opposite:
The architects replaced view-obstructing structural elements with soaring glass walls, which slide open to unite the interior with the dramatic Thunderbowl ski run.

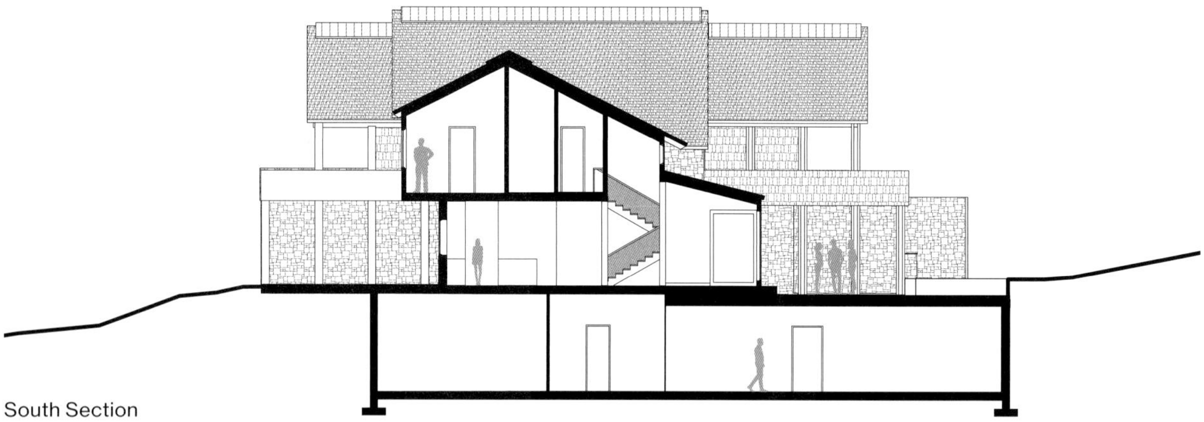

South Section

east. Part of opening up the floor plan was about allowing that light to balance as it comes through the house."

The biggest challenge, and the one that most engaged both the architects and their clients, was the second-floor primary suite, an ungainly bricolage of rooms extending the house's full width. The precinct, says Broughton, "was full of under-framing and structural articulation that didn't serve a purpose, cross-gables and dormers that were chopping up the ceiling on the inside." Though the problem proved so complicated that the architects had to build a model to decipher all the issues, they were eventually able to remove the visual clutter and craft a soaring, shaped ceiling. A low wall separating the sleeping and sitting areas, effectively a barrier, was extracted; part of an existing bathroom closet became a small office secreted behind a hidden door; and a new dressing area connects the bedroom to the expanded, almost entirely glazed bath, where glass panes in the trusses preserve light while sustaining acoustical privacy. What had been needlessly fussy and confusing stands now as a clean, volumetric experience—comfortable, useful, and elegant in its organic simplicity.

While R+B lightened the residence's overall palette, they also created a slight color distinction that codes the architecture. "All the beamwork, columns, and posts, all the doors and moldings, are original to the house, and they remain a dark cocoa," Broughton notes. Though the architects chose to bleach the existing floors and ceilings to foreground their texture and give them more presence, "all the wood we introduced is a lighter oak, so you can see the difference between old and new."

Injecting character and vitality into an existing house without gutting it—the standard gambit—requires a restraint born of humility, a recognition that even quotidian architecture can be distinctive and not require replacement. R+B, with their judicious surgical interventions, bestowed light, transparency, axiality, and an unmistakable overlay of pleasure, creating for a young family of four a true and lasting home. "This is a dream come true for them," says Broughton, "to be able at once to immerse themselves in nature and enjoy their own climbing wall and adventure rooms." The experience is as exhilarating as its incomparable alpine setting.

ANDRÉ FU

opposite and above:
The dining room features new floor-to-ceiling sliding glass doors that open the space to its natural surroundings. R+B's custom-designed and -crafted dining table was fitted with drawers abundant enough to hold children's crafts and games.

Throughout the preexisting house, R+B took every opportunity to remove structure, to open the spaces to the light and to each other. The opaque stair enclosure was replaced with translucent mesh (opposite), and a previously discrete den (above) became part of the kitchen.

opposite top:
The bunk room, on the house's lower level, sleeps four—children above, older siblings (or parents) below.

opposite bottom:
The recreation room can be configured for lounging, swinging, and climbing.

overleaf:
R+B simplified the architecture in the primary suite, shaping a warm series of soaring spaces at once grand in scale and intimate in character.

THE STUDIO

When we're asked to name our biggest project, we always have a ready reply: the firm. Probably a lot of architects would give the same answer, but the idea of what constitutes firm-building means different things to different practitioners. At R+B, we remain very aware that good work arises from meaningful collaborations, and great firms, along with great clients, are what in the end produce great buildings. Accordingly, we engage closely with the forty-plus teammates who make up the deep R+B bench, to ensure that each has a sense of meaningful participation in the studio's creations. Toward that end, we commit considerable time and attention to mentoring young talent and, especially, conveying the core values that define our sensibility: a passion for design excellence that puts a premium on originality and imagination; a commitment to honoring the trust of our clients with honesty, integrity, and accountability; and an understanding that, no matter how hard we all work, a balance between our professional and personal lives remains essential. Call it R+B's own particular interpretation of the Aspen Idea.

In fact, it would be hard to overstate how essential is a fine-grained involvement with our team, and how many different forms it takes. Continuing education, for instance: people emerging from design schools nowadays, we find, often lack a solid grounding in classical architecture, and so we remind young practitioners that, as innovative as Ludwig Mies van der Rohe was in his day, he tacked a drawing of a Greek column to the wall in every office he worked in. "You can't break the rules unless you know them" is a lesson we can't reiterate often enough.

We also coach up-and-coming architects on how to work with clients, how to ask meaningful questions in a way that will elicit useful responses. And we encourage our team not to be overly focused on outcomes but to embrace and enjoy the creative process and take the time to evolve beyond their first thoughts and early fixations. R+B doesn't have a rigid studio culture; neither of us has any expectations in that regard. Rather, we try to distill our experience into useful lessons, impart them with patience, and have faith that they will percolate.

Thinking about how best to evolve our practice leads us, inevitably, to ponder the meaning of the word. "Practice" is, of course, a simple definition applicable to any business, creative or otherwise: we have an architectural practice like a doctor has a medical practice. But "practice" also suggests something you do, day by day, to get better at your art or craft—to build on strengths, eliminate shortcomings, and discover new ideas and methodologies, in the same way that musicians practice to discover new techniques for extracting sound from an instrument, new riffs on familiar tunes, and new directions and movements. We also think of practice in terms of mindfulness, like a meditation practice that enables you—again, day by day—to be more completely in the moment, rather than ruminating about the past or agonizing over the future. In this respect, our practice most resembles our personal relationship. At home, we communicate our expectations but seldom hash things over—we make decisions quickly and contend with the consequences, positive or otherwise, as they arise. So it is at the studio: we work as we live, energetically and enthusiastically, in the moment.

R+B's Aspen and Denver studios both are designed to promote openness, ease of communication, and flow—of ideas as well as of people.

If there is a concept that sums up everything to which R+B aspires, it is sustainability. There is of course environmental sustainability, embodied by the triumvirate of carbon reduction; the resilience of systems that maximize a building's performance and enable it to evolve and adapt to changing environmental circumstances; and the well-being, both personal and planetary, that comes from natural, nontoxic materials. We also do a lot of remodeling: reusing the embodied energy in an existing structure is one of the greenest things an architect can do. But sustainability also applies to the creation of an enduring studio. Its essence, as noted, lies in mentoring our "family" and passing along R+B's core values. But it also has to do with the systems, both technological and human, that we put in place, the need to revisit and revise them, and to ensure that the decisions we made previously remain pertinent today and, indeed, in the foreseeable future. "Skate where the puck is going," we say. Sustainability, in effect, is readiness—anticipating what is to come, whatever that might be, and being prepared to receive it when it arrives.

R+B is at a juncture usually described as mid-career, and we're not generally inclined to do a lot of looking back. But when you decide to put your work between hard covers—a monograph!—you have to, and there's no denying that we've come quite a ways. When we first started the firm—out of our apartment, at the kitchen table—even though it was just the two of us, John started putting together a quality-control manual. "We're going to need this," he said. And R+B has been constantly evolving; the firm is very different from what it was even five years ago. So all that thinking ahead proved to be very useful indeed.

But one thing hasn't changed. It was encapsulated in a call we received from clients with two young children. A few weeks after they moved into their new house, they rang us up, in a state of semi-disbelief, to announce that their kids were so pleased with and proud of their new circumstances, they'd started making their beds. The story expresses R+B's most fundamental, inviolate belief: that good architecture can make you a better person, and the world a better place. That's what got us out of bed in the morning twenty years ago, and continues to exert its good influence, every day.

Game On

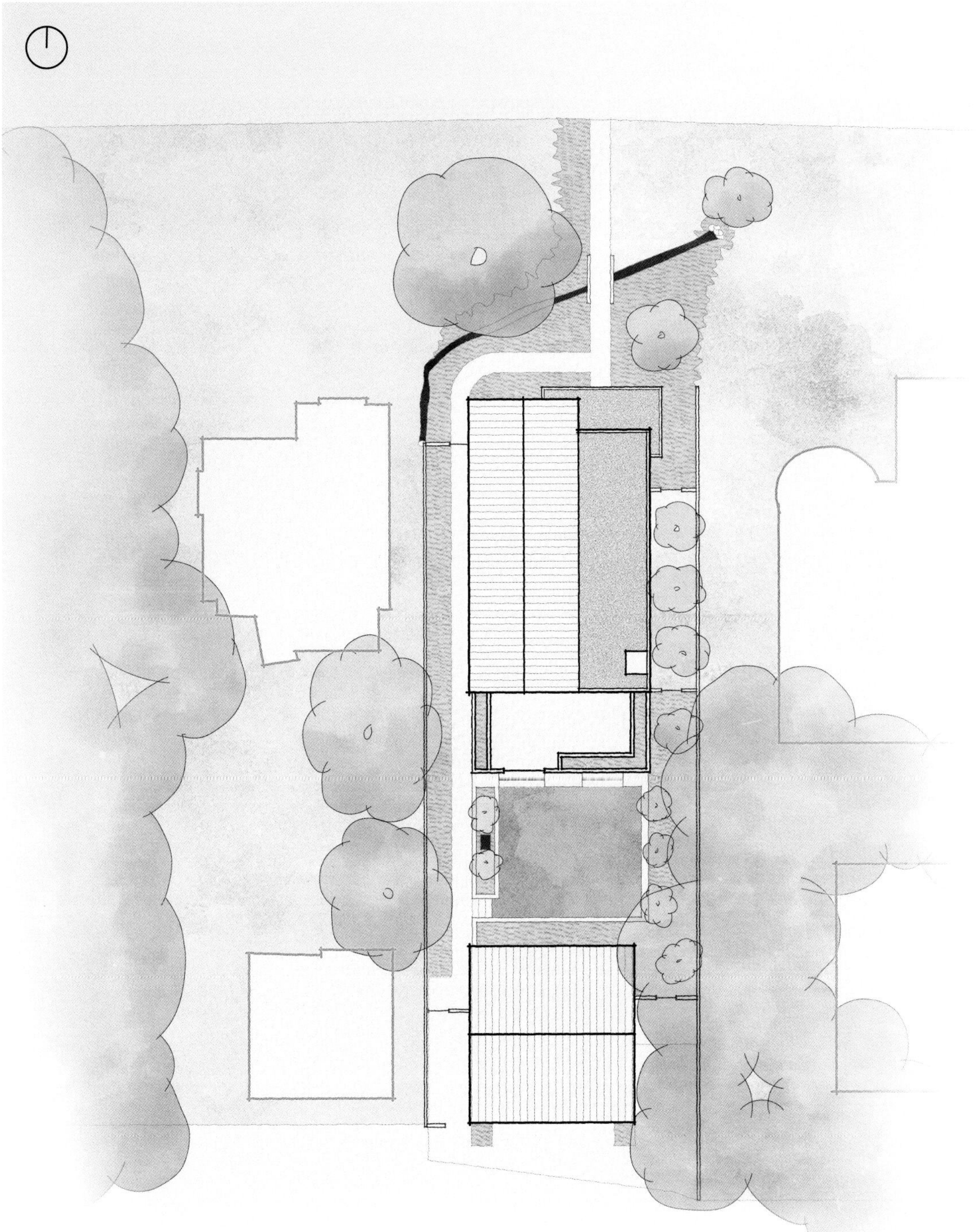

507

The idea of architecture that is contextual is, in a sense, double-edged. On the one hand, the decision to respect the aesthetic traditions of one's surroundings by not stridently contradicting them is laudable. On the other, contextualism can be the lazy creator's alibi for unimaginatively copying the neighbors. Champions of unfettered creativity, moreover, would argue—not unpersuasively—that you enrich, rather than diminish, a building's context with architecture that acknowledges no tradition but that of excellence.

Rowland+Broughton remain unambiguous contextualists, and find much to admire and appreciate in their West End neighborhood: a repository of (mostly) modest historic residences, some Victorian in character, many dating from the late nineteenth century, on suburban-scale lots. Yet their own home, the first they built from scratch—wittily named Game On, presumably for the couple's propensity to both work and play with astonishing focus and energy—manages to have it both ways. The design at once broadcasts its good-neighbor policy and subtly subverts it, with gestures that remain entirely personal and entirely of the moment.

Interestingly, the site was formerly occupied by the historic Victorian next door. The owner purchased the house, moved it to one side of the property, split the lot in two, and put the newly vacated eighth acre up for sale. "It was on the market forever," Rowland explains, "because people did not want to live across the street from a parking lot"—one that, while largely unused in winter, services the busy Aspen Music Festival and School Music Tent and Concert Hall in the summer. The absence of opposite neighbors, however, facilitated unobstructed views of Red Mountain, and the property was in close proximity to trails for hiking (one of the couple's passions) along and beyond Roaring Fork River. Not least, the couple could look across the street to the Boettcher Center (which they preserved) and the Resnick Center for Herbert Bayer Studies (for which R+B served as architect of record)—a pleasurable daily reminder of the firm's contributions to the community.

From the street, and at a glance, the house represents as the same vintage as the one beside it. Each shares three basic components: a projecting two-story gabled form, a subordinate side volume, slightly set back, and a front porch. But extend the glance, and the couple's residence leaps deftly forward in time, mostly notably via the Miesian cantilevered porch canopy and a slightly surreal decorative flourish: the architects continued the vertical and horizontal mullions of a second-story window the full width and height of the gabled volume, a gesture Rowland likens to a ribbon on a gift-wrapped package.

The main house comprises 3,300 square feet divided equally between three floors: a gym and massage room in the basement (easily convertible into two guest suites, should a future owner choose to do so); a main floor with a foyer and office in front and a kitchen/living/dining space on the house's garden side; and a primary suite and guest room upstairs. Without and within, the architecture reflects its influences. "When we were designing this house, we'd just come back from our first trip to Japan," Rowland recalls, "and we loved the spartan-ness of everything there, and the use of concrete. At the same time, we were designing a house on Cape Cod and were influenced by that regional vernacular—the modest volumes and surface articulation of the salt boxes and shingled cottages."

The interior is notable for an intriguing contrast: the restraint of its material palette, largely limited to concrete, white oak, and white-painted walls, and the gracious apportioning of space. The multivalent public room, lightly zoned into intercommunicating functions, distributes its square footage with a precise sense of how much is needed for each;

page 240:
John Rowland and Sarah Broughton's house at once acknowledges and contravenes the characteristics of its historic neighbors (note the Miesian cantilevered porch canopy).

opposite:
From the combination living/dining room to the covered sitting porch (with its kitchen elements) to the bocce court (on the other side of a raised fire pit), the back of the residence elegantly interleaves its experiential zones.

the primary suite comfortably embraces a large bedroom, a bath with a steam shower and cedar soaking tub, and a shared dressing closet with a washer and dryer, all without shortchanging the capacious guest suite; and there is a subterranean wellness center that is surprisingly spacious and well-equipped. It is not a big house. But it lives big, thanks to a finely tuned understanding on the part of Rowland+Broughton regarding what they wanted it to accomplish, and what was required to comfortably, effectively achieve that outcome.

That understanding extends to the outdoor zone, and in particular the elegance with which the architects connected it to the interior. Lift-and-slide floor-to-ceiling glass pocket doors open the entirety of the public space to a covered outdoor living room—fully furnished, and with a grilling station at one end—running the full width of the residence. Broad steps lead down to a gravel-covered bocce court that also serves as a storm-water filtration system. "All of the water that lands on the property finds its way into the bocce court, beneath which is seven feet of sand and fabric filters," says Rowland. "By the time it gets into the aquifer, which is directly below us, it's crystal clear." The court is flanked by concrete planters that soften the garden's edges with greenery and lightly screen the lot from the neighbors, contributing to the sense of privacy and peace that pervades the property.

Beyond the garden stands the 500-square-foot garage (accessed via an alleyway) and, beneath it, a comparably sized two-bedroom guest apartment, nicknamed Li'l G and typically inhabited by colleagues, friends, or team members visiting from R+B's Denver studio. Here, as in the main house, the spatial utility is remarkable. Within a small, below-grade footprint, Rowland+Broughton have comfortably arranged a fully equipped kitchen and sitting area, a grown-up bedroom, a bunkroom for kids, and a full bath. "People are always asking, 'Is Li'l G available?'" Rowland relates. "Somebody is there nearly all the time."

Perhaps unsurprisingly, the couple's dwelling also functions as a de facto design laboratory, where many components of the firm's major residential projects had their origins. The three most notable: the absence of hallways; the overscale pocket doors that maximize the indoor-outdoor interrelationship; and the projecting canopy (with integrated electric heating elements) that protects the outdoor living room and enhances its utility. Indeed, the couple often begin their workday here. "It's a satellite office," says Broughton, "where we can really jam."

Its modesty and simplicity (and LEED Gold rating) notwithstanding, the house remains unmistakably the lair of a pair of pleasure-loving sensualists, with a warm and welcoming vibe in an austere environment in the modern style. Perhaps for this reason—and unlike many practitioners, who prefer to keep work and life separate—Rowland+Broughton make a point of opening up their home for philanthropic gatherings and salon-style get-togethers. They also invite potential clients to drop in and have a look. "I think it's important to show them our own house," Broughton affirms, "not to encourage copying it, but to demonstrate a sensibility." Even so, Rowland adds, "When we once brought a couple here, they said, 'If you just do this for us, we'll be happy.'"

Jasper Johns: Mind/Mirror
Women Design
Libby Sellers
Modern Ikebana

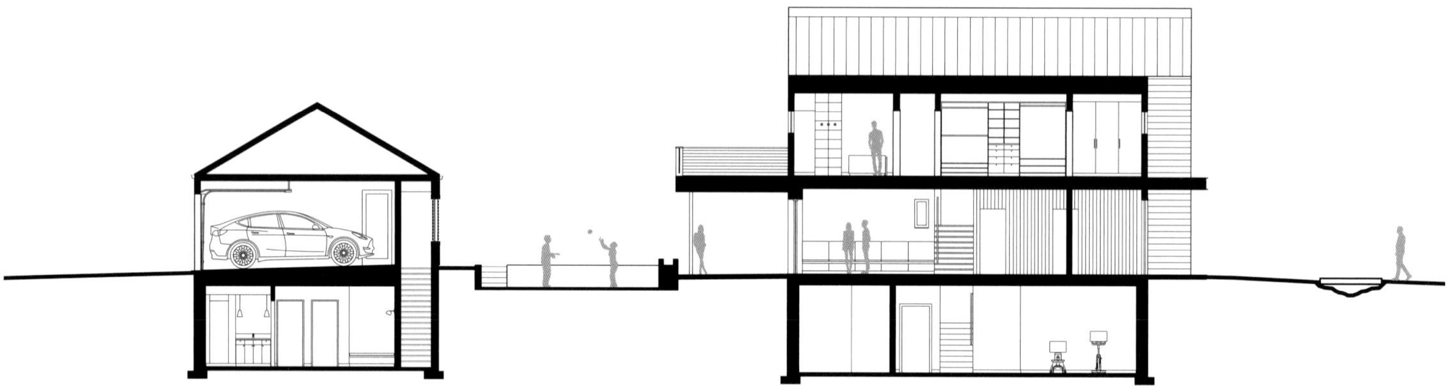

West Section

pages 244–45 and opposite: Many of the design ideas that find their way into R+B's projects originated in their own home—among them, fluent indoor/outdoor communication, exterior rooms that mirror their interior counterparts, exposed stairs, and open kitchens.

Acknowledgments

We are forever grateful to our clients, who are true visionaries, collaborators, and mentors. Their trust is exceptional, and they make us better through their leadership and friendship. Via the work and dedication of our amazing R+B team, whose perseverance is inspiring, dreams become reality. We are grateful as well to all of the creative partners, including fellow designers, engineers, and artists, with whom we join to create magic. Daring to take what we draw and make it reality is an exceptionally talented group of contractors and artisans who never say never. It is a persistent journey to create projects, and the relationships that arise from these efforts form the cherry atop the architectural confection.

We are honored that Princeton Architectural Press has given us this opportunity to share our projects and our view of Aspen. We are so thankful for the people who have worked passionately to bring this book to life, both internally and externally. The team at Princeton Architectural Press have been awesome partners and tirelessly encouraging of our efforts. Jill Cohen and her associate Melissa Powell have given unwavering guidance. Marc Kristal's prose has captured our work so eloquently. Our graphic designer and photographers have presented our inspirations and work with clarity and beauty.

And lastly, we must acknowledge our great muse: Aspen. To our neighbors and friends, city officials, and city staff who remain dedicated to keeping Aspen meaningful, thank you for your loyalty and support. We are forever indebted to the wholehearted embrace that has been given to us by the community. We continually strive to raise the bar and to be good stewards of our hometown.

Credits

All photography by Lisa Romerein except the following:
David Marlow: 21
Joshua McHugh: 4–5, 156–71, 176–77, 182–93, 196–97
Brent Moss: 248–49
Shawn O'Connor: 19

All projects styled by Helen Crowther except Art Barn and Bagua

Art Barn

Team: John Rowland, AIA, principal in charge; Sarah Broughton, FAIA, NCIDQ, principal; Amanda Christianson, AIA, project manager; Bryan May, AIA; Craig Lawrence, AIA; Brandt Schwayder; Katie King; R+B team members
Interiors: Atelier AM
Consultants: KL&A Structural Engineers (structural engineer); Resource Engineering Group (MEP engineer); Shannon Murphy Landscape Architects (landscape architect); Elumenate (lighting design); Paragon Systems Integration (A/V); WorldStage (video art consultant); Alexandre Avdulov, John McGee (tea masters)
Contractor: Hansen Construction

Bagua

Team: John Rowland, AIA, principal in charge; Sarah Broughton, FAIA, NCIDQ, principal; Bryan May, AIA, project manager; Brett Lohr; R+B team members
Interiors: Terri Ricci Interiors
Consultants: KL&A Structural Engineers (structural engineer); Architectural Engineering Consultants (MEP engineer); Land Design 39 (landscape architect); LEAX (lighting design)
Contractor: Schlumberger Scherer Construction

Barn Studio

Team: Sarah Broughton, FAIA, principal in charge; John Rowland, AIA, principal; Sara Upton, AIA, project manager; Will Otte, AIA; R+B team members
Interiors: Rowland+Broughton
Consultants: KL&A Structural Engineers (structural engineer); Resource Engineering Group (MEP engineer); HLB Lighting Design (lighting designer)
Contractor: Schlumberger Scherer Construction

Creek House

Team: Sarah Broughton, FAIA, principal in charge; John Rowland, AIA, principal; Sara Upton, AIA, project manager; Will Otte, AIA; R+B team members
Interiors: Samantha Crasco and Sarah Collum-Hatfield
Consultants: KL&A Structural Engineers (structural engineer); Resource Engineering Group (MEP Engineer); Land Design 39 landscape architect); HLB Lighting Design (lighting design)
Contractor: Independence Construction Group

Game On

Team: John Rowland, AIA, principal in charge; Sarah Broughton, FAIA, NCIDQ, principal; Dana Ellis, AIA, project manager; Amanda Christianson, AIA; Jayna Barber, NCIDQ; R+B team members
Interiors: Rowland+Broughton
Consultants: KL&A Structural Engineers (structural engineer); BG Buildingworks (MEP engineer); Elements (landscape architect)
Contractor: Schlumberger Scherer Construction

Lookout House

Team: Sarah Broughton, FAIA, principal in charge; John Rowland, AIA, principal; Delvon Nemechek, AIA, project manager; R+B team members
Interiors: Manuel de Santaren; Rowland+Broughton
Consultants: KL&A Structural Engineers (structural engineer); Rader Engineering (MEP engineer); Rowland+Broughton (landscape design); Robert Singer Associates (lighting designer)
Contractor: Brikor Associates

Meadow House

Team: Sarah Broughton, FAIA, NCIDQ, principal in charge; John Rowland, AIA, principal; Sara Upton, AIA, project manager; Mark Bever, AIA; Will Otte, AIA; Carrera Shea, NCIDQ; Derek Keil, AIA; R+B team members
Interiors: Rowland+Broughton
Consultants: Albright & Associates (structural engineer); Resource Engineering Group (MEP engineer); Robert Singer & Associates (lighting designer)
Contractor: Schlumberger Scherer Construction

Mountain Retreat

Team: Sarah Broughton, FAIA, principal in charge; John Rowland, AIA, principal; Sara Upton, AIA, project manager; Will Otte, AIA; Mark Hardeman; Carrera Shea, NCIDQ; Leslie Cope, NCIDQ; Rahul Mohare; R+B team members
Interiors: Rowland+Broughton
Consultants: KL&A Structural Engineers (structural engineer); BG Buildingworks (MEP engineer); Design Workshop (landscape architect); Mitchell B. Kohn Lighting Design (lighting design)
Contractor: RA Nelson

Ridge House

Team: Sarah Broughton, FAIA, NCIDQ, principal in charge; John Rowland, AIA, principal; Sara Upton, AIA, project manager; Will Otte, AIA; Mark Bever, AIA; R+B team members
Interiors: Rowland+Broughton
Consultants: KL&A Structural Engineers (structural engineer); Resource Engineering Group (MEP engineer); HLB Lighting Design (lighting designer)
Contractor: Schlumberger Scherer Construction

Thunderbowl

Team: Sarah Broughton, FAIA, principal in charge; John Rowland, AIA, principal; Leslie Cope, NCIDQ; Caroline Dini; Brooke Pisani; R+B team members
Interiors: Rowland+Broughton
Consultants: Oddo Engineering (structural engineer); Rader Engineering (MEP engineer); Aspen Valley Landscaping (landscaping); HLB Lighting Design (lighting designer)
Contractor: Schlumberger Scherer Construction